NOW YOU KNOW

KNOW

FOOTBALL

NOW YOU KNOW

KNOW

FOOTBALL

Doug Lennox

DUNDURN PRESS
TORONTO

Editor: Barry Jowett
Copy Editor: Cheryl Hawley
Design: Courtney Horner
Printer: Webcom

Library and Archives Canada Cataloguing in Publication

Lennox, Doug
            Now you know football / by Doug Lennox.

ISBN 978-1-55488-453-7

            1. Football--Miscellanea. I. Title.

GV950.5.L46 2009   796.33202   C2009-902996-0

1   2   3   4   5   13   12   11   10   09

Canada I+I

Conseil des Arts
du Canada

Canada Council
for the Arts

ONTARIO ARTS COUNCIL
CONSEIL DES ARTS DE L'ONTARIO

We acknowledge the support of The Canada Council for the Arts and the Ontario Arts Council for our publishing program. We also acknowledge the financial support of the Government of Canada through the Book Publishing Industry Development Program and The Association for the Export of Canadian Books, and the Government of Ontario through the Ontario Book Publishers Tax Credit program, and the Ontario Media Development Corporation.

Care has been taken to trace the ownership of copyright material used in this book. The author and the publisher welcome any information enabling them to rectify any references or credits in subsequent editions.

J. Kirk Howard, President

www.dundurn.com

Dundurn Press	Gazelle Book Services Limited	Dundurn Press
3 Church Street, Suite 500	White Cross Mills	2250 Military Road
Toronto, Ontario, Canada	High Town, Lancaster, England	Tonawanda, NY
M5E 1M2	LA1 4XS	U.S.A. 14150

contents

preface

Football enjoys massive popularity in the United States and Canada, but has also gained followers around the world. The game's popularity probably has a lot to do with the fact that once a week a football game becomes the focus of a community.

Other great sports are also popular, but sports like hockey and basketball are played three or four times a week, while baseball is played almost every day. Most fans watch some games, but not all.

When a sport has only one game a week, like football, the entire fan base — from the most devoted to the most casual of fans — is fully focused around that one game. And at work or at school on Monday, the guy who paints a team logo on his exposed stomach and the woman who puts war paint on her face can talk about the same game and the same plays with the guy or girl who saw parts of the game on TV between commercial breaks of a weekend-afternoon movie.

Football is about stories: those stories we relive with friends who experienced them with us, or stories we tell to others who weren't there to see that great catch or game-turning interception.

And that's really what this book is. It's stories. It's not a book of quizzes with true/false or multiple-choice answers. This, like all the *Now You Know* books, answers each question with a brief, easily digestible story. Some will be stories familiar to the reader, but most will be new. And even those familiar stories might contain a fascinating bit of information you never knew before (or had forgotten).

So, it's my hope that this little book adds to your enjoyment of this great sport, and gives you a few more stories that you can enjoy during that long week between games.

Enjoy!

gridiron history

Who was the first professional football player?

In the early days of the sport, football games were contested by amateurs and rules forbade teams from paying athletes. Some athletic clubs got around such rules by securing jobs for star players or awarding gifts, such as expensive watches, which the athletes would then pawn.

On November 12, 1892, the Allegheny Athletic Association football team took on their bitter rivals, the Pittsburgh Athletic Club. PAC approached William "Pudge" Heffelfinger, a player from Chicago, and offered him $250 to play a single game for their team. AAA caught wind of the offer, and also approached Heffelfinger. Heffelfinger was unwilling to risk his amateur status for $250, so AAA offered $500. Heffelfinger accepted, and scored the only touchdown of the game on a 25-yard fumble return.

The next year, AAA became more thoroughly "professional" by paying a trio of players — Peter Wright, James Van Cleve, and Oliver Rafferty — $50 each per game.

How much did it cost to be a charter member of the National Football League?

In 1920, 11 football clubs joined forces to form the American Professional Football Association. The legendary Jim Thorpe was named the league's first president. Franchise fees were low on the priority list for the new league, but for the sake of putting a figure on paper, membership in the APFA was set at $100 per team.

The setting of a fee was a mere formality. No team ever actually paid the fee, and so, in reality, joining the league was free.

The APFA later changed its name to the National Football League.

When was the first NFL game played?

After the formation of the American Professional Football Association (later renamed the NFL) in August and September of 1920, the first team to see action was the Rock Island, Illinois franchise, the Independents. The game, on September 25, 1920, was played before a crowd of 800 fans, and saw the Independents hammer their opponents, the St. Paul Ideals (NOT a member of the APFA), 48–0.

The first game between two APFA/NFL teams occurred a week later on October 3. Dayton defeated Columbus, 14–0.

What short-lived NFL franchise was known for their halftime show, which featured dog stunts, and a player wrestling a bear?

With fewer than 1,000 residents, LaRue, Ohio, was the smallest town to ever be the base of an NFL team, so it's not surprising that their team, the Oorang Indians, only played one "home" game in their two-year history. In fact, that one game had to be played in nearby Marion, Ohio, as LaRue did not have a football field.

The Indians were simply a marketing venture for William Lingo, owner of the Oorang Dog Kennels. The team, which first took the field in 1922, was made up of Native American players, most notably Jim Thorpe.

As a marketing venture, the success of the team on the score sheet was of little importance. Lingo simply wanted to draw attention to his kennels. To that end, he developed a popular halftime show that featured his dogs performing stunts, as well as demonstrations of Native dances and rituals. One of the Indians players, Nikolas Lassa, had experience as a wrestler and put those skills to use by wrestling a bear at some halftime shows, to the delight of the audience.

Quickies

Did you know ...

- That the first professional football game played at the Rose Bowl in Pasadena was Super Bowl XI? The Oakland Raiders defeated the Minnesota Vikings, 32–14.
- That Super Bowl XI was the last Super Bowl to finish during daylight hours?
- That Super Bowl XI was played on January 9, 1977 — the earliest a Super Bowl has ever been played. The regular season had started a week earlier than usual to avoid playoff games falling on Christmas Day.

Like most novelties, however, the novelty of the Oorang Indians and their halftime show wore off. After a 1–10 season in 1923, the team folded.

Who was the Super Bowl trophy named after?

While the game itself is known as the Super Bowl, the NFL's championship trophy is called the Vince Lombardi Trophy.

Vince Lombardi was the legendary coach of the Green Bay Packers from 1959 to 1967. He coached the Packers to five NFL Championships, and two Super Bowls. His career playoff record was 9–1, while his regular season record was 96–34–6.

Vince Lombardi later joined the Washington Redskins in 1969, but after one season was diagnosed with colon cancer and passed away in September 1970, at the age of 57.

A week later, the NFL changed the name of its ultimate prize from the "World Championship Game Trophy" to the "Vince Lombardi Trophy."

Who called Super Bowl III Joe Namath's "first professional football game"?

When the New York Jets earned a spot in the AFL-NFL Championship Game in 1969, few gave the AFL champs a chance. They were, after all, facing the Baltimore Colts, who were being touted as the greatest team of all time. The AFL, meanwhile, was considered by most to be the far weaker of the two leagues. Many scoffed when Joe Namath famously guaranteed that the Jets would win the game.

The harshest criticism came from Norm Van Brocklin, a former player and coach who would be inducted into the Pro Football Hall of Fame in 1971. Brocklin dismissed the AFL with the cutting remark, "This will be Namath's first professional football game."

The Jets stunned Brocklin, the Colts, and the football world with a 16–7 victory.

How many American cities have fielded teams in the CFL?

Quickies
Did you know ...
- That several American states have more than one NFL team, but only two states have three teams? Those states are: California (Oakland, San Diego, and San Francisco) and Florida (Jacksonville, Miami, and Tampa)

In total, seven American cities have been part of the CFL.

In the 1990s, the CFL embarked on a grand experiment to expand into the United States. The first U.S. based team, the Sacramento Gold Miners, took the field in 1993. The following season they were joined by teams in Baltimore, Las Vegas, and Shreveport, Louisiana. By 1995, the expansion was struggling, and the Las Vegas team folded, while the Sacramento team moved to San Antonio. Other teams were added in Memphis and Birmingham, Alabama, with little success.

After two seasons of American expansion, all but the Baltimore Stallions and San Antonio Texans had called it quits. The Stallions — upon learning that the NFL's Cleveland Browns were moving to Baltimore — relocated to Montreal, becoming the latest incarnation of the Alouettes. The Texans, unenthused at the prospects of playing the lone American team in a league based in a country more than 1,500 miles away, ceased operations.

How many times have NFL and CFL teams squared off?

During the 1950s and 1960s, there were several attempts to pit NFL/AFL teams against CFL teams in exhibition games north of the border. The games were played with mixed rules — one half would be played under American rules, the other under Canadian rules.

The first games were played in 1950 and 1951, when the New York Giants travelled to Ottawa to play the Rough Riders.

Later in the decade, the exhibition games were revived, with single games in 1959 and 1960, and three games in 1961.

American teams won all but one of the games — the exception being the 1961 tilt that saw the Hamilton Tiger-Cats defeat the AFL's Buffalo Bills 38–21.

Results of Games Between CFL and NHL/AFL Teams:
- 1950: New York Giants (NFL) 20, Ottawa Rough Riders 6
- 1951: New York Giants (NFL) 38, Ottawa Rough Riders 6
- 1959: Chicago Cardinals (NFL) 55, Toronto Argonauts 26
- 1960: Pittsburgh Steelers (NFL) 43, Toronto Argonauts 26
- 1961: St. Louis Cardinals (NFL) 36, Toronto Argonauts 7
- 1961: Chicago Bears (NFL) 34, Montreal Alouetts 16
- 1961: Hamilton Tiger-Cats 38, Buffalo Bills (AFL) 21

What CFL team played without a name during its first season?

When the city of Baltimore was granted a CFL franchise for the 1994 season, owner Jim Speros wanted to name the team the Baltimore Colts — which was the name of the city's original NFL franchise. The NFL, which held the rights to the name, took legal action, winning an injunction.

Stuck without a name, the team was referred to as the Baltimore CFLers and the Baltimore Football Club, but had no official name. As an act of defiance, the team's public address announcer would introduce the team as "Your Baltimore ..." allowing the spectators to shout out "Colts."

After the season, fans were given a chance to vote for a new name for the team. The winning name was "Stallions."

Which came first, the Ottawa Rough Riders or the Saskatchewan Roughriders?

It was long a source of amusement that the CFL had two teams with nearly identical names — the Rough Riders and the Roughriders. Both claimed to be the "true" Riders, but Ottawa was the first to use the name.

The Ottawa team was first established in 1876 as a member of the Ontario Amateur Athletic Association. For 21 years it played nameless, until adopting the name "Rough Riders" in 1897. The name was a reference to the log rollers who would ride the logs on the rough local rivers.

By the 1920s, East-West matches were commonplace and the Regina Rugby Club took the field in 1921. Three years later, the Ottawa franchise changed their name to the Senators, and the Regina club snatched the name, squeezing it into one word, *Roughriders*. (There are two theories about the origins of their version of the name: one theory contends the

Regina team named themselves after the North-West Mounted Police, who were known as "roughriders" for their ability to break wild horses; the other argues that the team was named after a Canadian regiment that fought in the Spanish-American War.)

They played as the Regina Roughriders until 1948, when teams in Moose Jaw and Saskatoon folded and the Regina team came under the ownership of the province. Since then, they have been known as the Saskatchewan Roughriders.

What were the four traditional New Year's Day bowl games?

Before the days of the Bowl Championship Series, New Year's Day was college football's biggest day, often with multiple games that had National Championship implications.

College bowl games in the United States have a tradition dating back to the original bowl game, the 1902 Rose Bowl. Originally the Rose Bowl was the only major college bowl game. In the mid-1930s, it was joined by the Sugar Bowl, the Orange Bowl, and the Cotton Bowl.

For many years these games were played almost exclusively on New Year's Day, until BCS scheduling made it necessary to break up the tradition.

Where did the Cleveland Browns get their name?

When Cleveland was granted membership in the All-America Football Conference in 1945, they held a public contest to name the team. Initially, fans selected the name "Panthers," but the rights to that name were owned by a local businessman who owned a semi-pro team with the same name. The fans were polled again, and this time the most popular submission was "Browns," in honour of the team's popular coach, general manager, and vice-president, Paul Brown.

Brown was already a local legend, having coached the Ohio State Buckeyes to a National Championship in 1942. After military duty in World War II, rather than return to Ohio State, Brown accepted the position with the Cleveland team in the new All-America Football Conference. The league was set to begin play in the 1946 season as a rival to the National Football League.

Brown was bashful about having the team named after himself, and told the media that "Browns" was short for "Brown Bombers," in honour of legendary heavyweight boxer Joe Louis. However, whether he liked it or not, he was the team's namesake.

How did the "Super Bowl" get its name?

When the AFL and NFL merged, they agreed to meet in a championship game every season. Lamar Hunt — owner of the Kansas City Chiefs and founder of the AFL — jokingly referred to the game as the "Super Bowl." Hunt was playing on the name of a popular toy at the time — the extra-bouncy Super Ball.

Fans and media, preferring the ad-libbed name to the cumbersome official title — the AFL-NFL World Championship Game — used the shortened version instead. By the time the third championship rolled around in 1969, the name had been made official. The first two games were retroactively renamed Super Bowls I and II.

Who was the Grey Cup named after?

Albert Henry George Grey, fourth Earl Grey, was governor general of Canada from 1904 to 1911. In 1909 he sought to cement his legacy by donating a sports trophy.

Originally, the plan was to award the Grey Cup to the champion amateur senior hockey team in the country. However, Sir H. Allan Montagu got in the way by donating the Allan Cup — a trophy still awarded to this day. The Grey Cup was then designated for the amateur rugby football champion.

Unfortunately, Earl Grey was a little slow about getting the trophy ready. When the University of Toronto won the first Grey Cup game that December, no trophy was present. The championship team was not awarded the Grey Cup until March 1910.

When was the first Pro Bowl played?

Prior to the inception of the Pro Bowl, the NFL had staged all-star games. The first came after the 1938–39 season and pitted the New York Giants against a team of all-stars. It was a one-time event — there was no all-star game the following years.

In 1951, the idea was reborn and reformatted, with conference all-stars squaring off. The AFL staged all-star games of their own beginning in 1962.

After the AFL and NFL merged, the modern-day Pro Bowl was created. The first true Pro Bowl was played at the Los Angeles Memorial Coliseum on January 24, 1971. The NFC defeated the AFC 27–6.

When was the first night football game played?

Mansfield, Pennsylvania, was abuzz with excitement over the 1892 Great Mansfield Fair. The excitement was not about the planned game between the Mansfield Normal School football team and the visiting Wyoming Seminary. Rather, people were eager to see the area's first ever demonstration of electric lighting. The Mansfield team had arranged to play the first-ever night game. Football itself was something of a novelty for the Mansfield squad — this would be only their fifth game, day or night.

Unfortunately, the first attempt to illuminate a football game was a resounding failure. Because lighting in the 1890s was not as powerful as it would later become, the field was poorly lit. To make matters worse, some of the lights were mounted on a pole at midfield.

At the end of the first half, with limited visibility, teams failing to attain first downs, and players unable to determine which team had the ball, the game was halted and declared a 0–0 tie.

How many times has the CFL staged an All-Star Game?

The CFL All-Star Game has had an on-again, off-again existence since the 1950s. The game was played for four consecutive years, from 1955 to 1958, and then shelved. It was reborn in 1970 and had a steady run until 1978.

Two attempts were made to revive the game. In 1983, the Eastern and Western conferences squared off at B.C. Place in Vancouver. In 1988, the league experimented with a format they'd tried in the early seventies, matching the Grey Cup champions (the Edmonton Eskimos) against a team of league all-stars.

In total, fourteen all-star games have been played. While the game is no longer held, the CFL now releases an annual list of all-stars.

Did Deion Sanders play in an NFL game and a Major League Baseball game on the same day?

In the 1990s Deion Sanders managed to play both football and baseball professionally, but was confronted with the same problem every season: the end of the Major League Baseball season overlaps with the beginning of the NFL season. In 1992, Sanders was a member of both the Atlanta Braves and the Atlanta Falcons. The Braves were headed for the playoffs, and Sanders elected to stick with his baseball team. The Falcons fined him $68,000 for missing the first games of the season. So, in a desire to appease his football team and make history at the same time, Sanders attempted to play two games on one day.

It would have been easier had both teams been playing in Atlanta that day. Instead, he travelled to Miami for an afternoon game between the Falcons and Dolphins, then flew to Pittsburgh for a National League Championship Series game between the Braves and Pirates in the evening.

Urban legend has it that Sanders played in both games that day. Unfortunately for the legend, and for Deion, Braves manager Bobby Cox did not play Sanders that night.

How many games were played with replacement players during the 1987 NFL season?

In 1987, the National Football League Players' Association went on strike for the second time in six seasons. While the first strike, in 1982, had resulted in the league going dark for nearly two months, the second strike prompted a response from owners that the union had not anticipated: they continued to play using replacement players.

The replacement players were largely former college players and castoffs from training camp. Much to the chagrin of the union, not only were teams able to fill their rosters with these players, but network television continued to broadcast the games.

Player support for the strike eroded, and 89 union members crossed the picket line. After three weeks and 42 games of replacement football, the strike ended without a new collective bargaining agreement.

The union was subsequently decertified and continued to operate as a professional association. In 1993, the NFLPA reconstituted itself as a labour union.

What is the oldest trophy in football?

While the Little Brown Jug is perhaps the best known ancient piece of football hardware — going to the winner of games between Michigan and Minnesota in the NCAA every year since 1903 — it is not the oldest.

The oldest football trophy still in use is the Yates Cup. Established in 1898, the Yates Cup was awarded to the champion of the Senior Intercollegiate Football League until 1971, when it became the championship football trophy of the Ontario University Athletics Association (now known as Ontario University Athletics).

> **Quickies**
> *Did you know ...*
> • James Naismith, the inventor of basketball, is sometimes credited with inventing the original football helmet?

Why did one state's attorney general investigate the Bowl Championship Series for antitrust violations?

In the 2008 NCAA football season, the Utah Utes went 13–0, including a 31–17 victory over Alabama in the Sugar Bowl. As the only undefeated team in the country, many felt they were deserving of a National Championship. However, the Utes play in the Mountain West conference, which does not have an automatic berth into bowl games and is not eligible for the BCS title game.

Utah attorney general Mark Shurtleff, one of many in the state unhappy with the oversight of the Utes, launched an investigation to determine whether the BCS system unfairly favours the "big" conference schools. As of press time, Shurtleff was still considering pursuing the matter further.

Quickies

Did you know ...
* That during World War II there was a shortage of men to play professional sports, so military units often competed instead? Between 1942 and 1944, Grey Cup games were contested between service teams.

Why do early references to the Canadian game call it "rugby football"?

While rugby had been played in Canada from the mid-1900s, the game developed and a hybrid known as "rugby football" became the dominant form of the sport in Canada. The Canadian game, in fact, came to resemble the modern version of football.

American schools changed their game of football after seeing how Canadians played rugby. Then the Americans made changes that influenced the Canadian game. Most notably, instead of beginning play with a scrum, the new version of the game began play with a snap, and teams had to attain a certain number of yards in order to retain possession.

For many years, this brand of football was known as "rugby football" in Canada, and leagues and championships referred to it as such. Eventually, the word "rugby" fell out of common use, as the game became too distinct from the British sport.

Who was the model for the Heisman Trophy?

The trophy, originally known as the Downtown Athletic Club Trophy, was sculpted by Frank Eliscu. Although members of the Fordham football team helped to perfect the pose depicted by the trophy, the original model was Ed Smith, who played for New York University.

The trophy was first awarded in 1935. In 1936, it was renamed the Heisman Memorial Trophy in honour of the Downtown Athletic Club's late director, John Heisman.

How many Eastern Division Championships have the Winnipeg Blue Bombers won?

Though traditionally a Western team, major changes have led to the Winnipeg Blue Bombers playing the CFL's Eastern Division on numerous occasions.

After the collapse of the Montreal Allouettes in 1987, the league moved the Bombers from the West to the East in order to avoid a three-team Eastern Division. Football returned to Montreal in 1995, and the Bombers moved back to the West. Their stay didn't last long, however, as the Ottawa Rough Riders folded and Winnipeg became an Eastern Division city again in 1997.

Ottawa briefly returned to the CFL with the Renegades from 2002 to 2005, causing another shift back to the West, but the failure of that franchise led to the return of Winnipeg to the East in 2006.

During their time as an Eastern Division team, the Winnipeg Blue Bombers have won seven division championships, in 1987, 1990, 1992, 1993, 2001, and 2007. Only one of those championships — in 1990 — was converted into a Grey Cup championship.

What major brewery named its most popular beer after a football team?

Labatt's cornerstone beer began life in the early 1950s as "Labatt's

Pilsener Lager." But the beer's distinct blue label led Winnipeg Blue Bombers fans to calling the beer "Blue" after their football team. The name eventually stuck, and became the official name of the brew, which is one of the bestselling beers in Canada.

Labatt's later became affiliated with another "Blue" team as the original owners of the Toronto Blue Jays. Unfortunately for the Labatt's marketing department, both "Blue" teams are commonly referred to by the colourless short-forms of their names: the Bombers and the Jays.

When did the AFL and NFL become the AFC and NFC?

On June 8, 1966, the heated rivalry between the National Football League and the American Football League came to an end as the two leagues agreed to merge into one mighty National Football League.

The agreement called for a gradual merger that saw both leagues continue under their original names for a few years, meeting in an annual AFL-NFL Championship Game (later known as the Super Bowl) at season's end.

After expansions and realignments, the merger was finally completed in 1970, and the old AFL and NFL became known as the American Football Conference and the National Football Conference.

What coach lost a National Championship in 1984 by electing to go for a two-point conversion?

Tom Osborne, who built a perennial powerhouse in the Nebraska Cornhuskers, made a decision that was debated for years afterward at the 1984 Orange Bowl.

The Huskers came into the game 12–0, and ranked first in the nation. They were expected to be named National Champions with a win or a tie, but the underdog University of Miami team managed to grab a 31–17 lead by the fourth quarter. The Huskers scored twice, and after the second touchdown were faced with a tough decision: kick the single point for the tie and a National Championship, or go for two to win the game outright.

Osborne, believing that you play football games to win, not to tie, elected to go for two points. The play was broken up, and the Huskers lost the game. Miami was subsequently named National Champions.

Who owned the Hamilton Tiger-Cats and the Toronto Maple Leafs?

Torontonians already had a dislike for Harold Ballard, whose ownership of hockey's Toronto Maple Leafs had been, and would remain, chaotic and controversial for years. Then, in 1978, Ballard bought the fledgling Hamilton Tiger-Cats — the hated rivals of the Toronto Argonauts. To make matters worse, the Tiger-Cats under Ballard appeared in four Grey Cups, winning once, while the Toronto Maple Leafs were in the middle of a prolonged Stanley Cup drought.

Not that Hamiltonians were any more fond of Ballard and his antics. He once referred to the Tiger-Cats as a "bunch of overpaid losers." Later that year — after the Tiger-Cats won the Grey Cup — he admitted that they were "worth every penny."

When was the first NFL Draft?

Though he would later be commissioner of the NFL, Bert Bell was owner of the Philadelphia Eagles in 1935 when he proposed that the owners institute a draft system that would allow weaker teams to have the first choice of players eligible to enter the league. The other owners agreed, and on February 8, 1936, the first ever NFL draft was held at the Ritz-Carlton Hotel in New York City.

Bell's plan seemed to work in his favour, as his Eagles used the first pick in the draft to select the first Heisman Trophy winner, Jay Berwanger. Unfortunately for the Eagles, Berwanger was not nearly as keen on professional football as the Eagles were on him. He decided that there was no money in football, and never played in the NFL.

Who signed with the Toronto Argonauts prior to the 1991 NFL Draft?

Notre Dame wide receiver Raghib "Rocket" Ismail had a stellar final season of collegiate football in 1990. He finished second in the Heisman Trophy voting, and was projected to be chosen first overall in the NFL Draft.

But while the Dallas Cowboys, who held the number one pick, awaited their chance to select Ismail, the Toronto Argonauts were courting him behind the scenes. The team's new ownership group — made up of Bruce McNall, movie star John Candy, and hockey legend Wayne Gretzky — was looking to make a splash, and snatching the coveted Ismail seemed to be the way to do it.

On the day of the NFL Draft, the Argos announced that they had signed Ismail to a four-year, $18.2 million contract. Ismail subsequently fell to number 100 in the draft.

Where was the first documented game of football played?

While football has become one of America's greatest passions, and one of its great sports exports, the first documented game played in North America was played at the University of Toronto in 1861.

Eight years later, the game had reached the United States; Rutgers and Princeton squared off in the first known contest of a game called "football" between American colleges.

Though the early form of the game in North America was a distant ancestor of the modern game, these contests helped to establish football as a staple of college sports.

What was the Hampden Park Blood Bath?

The annual Yale-Harvard football game has always been intense, but in the 1890s the rivalry was so heated that the games were often violent.

There was so much animosity that on the night before the 1894 encounter, Yale's coach advised his players to make illegal hits, regardless of what penalties were doled out.

The game was one of the most violent ever played. Several players took serious blows to the head, two were jabbed in the eye causing bleeding, legs and noses were broken, and one player, Fred Murphy, was in a coma for several hours. After the game, fans of both teams took the fight to the streets.

The public outcry resulted in the game being suspended until 1897.

What stadium was the model for the Rose Bowl?

Architect Myron Hunt's design for the Rose Bowl has achieved iconic status and helped to make the stadium one of the most famous in college football.

But the design was not completely original. The Yale Bowl, home to the Yale Bulldogs, was Hunt's inspiration. Though the Rose Bowl's fame continues, thanks in large part to the annual game that shares its name, the Yale Bowl has become a much less-known facility outside the Ivy League.

How many teams have gone undefeated in the NFL?

Four teams have finished the NFL's regular season with perfect records: the 1934 Chicago Bears (13–0), the 1942 Chicago Bears (11–0), the 1972 Miami Dolphins (14–0), and the 2007 New England Patriots (16–0).

However, completing a perfect season that includes a championship has proven to be a far more difficult task. Both Bears teams lost the NFL Championship Game, while the Patriots suffered a last-minute defeat at the hands of the underdog New York Giants.

The 1972 Dolphins, who defeated the Washington Redskins 14–7 in Super Bowl VII, have completed the only truly perfect season in NFL history.

How many teams have gone undefeated in the CFL?

Perfect seasons have been tough to come by in the CFL, particularly in the modern era of 20-game seasons. Only one team has pulled off a perfect season in CFL history, and even that perfection is debatable.

The 1948 Calgary Stampeders finished the regular season with a 12–0 record. At the time, Calgary was a member of the Western Interprovincial Football Union, which played its championships under a two-game total-points format. The teams tied the first game, 4–4, and Calgary won the second, 21–10. While the tie would seem to mar the perfect record, the total-points format meant that neither game could be considered a win, loss, or tie on its own.

Following the win, Calgary went on to the Grey Cup and defeated the Ottawa Roughriders, 12–7.

How many teams have gone undefeated in CIS/CIAU?

Canada's university football organization, now known as Canadian Interuniversity Sports, and formerly known as the Canadian Interuniversity Athletic Union, has seen only one team finish with a perfect regular season and go on to win the Vanier Cup. The 2007 Manitoba Bisons accomplished this feat when they defeated the St. Mary's Huskies 28–14 to finish the year with a perfect 12–0 record.

Why did Theodore Roosevelt threaten to ban football?

Quickies
Did you know ...
- Washington University holds the NCAA Division I FBS record for the longest undefeated streak. In 63 games between 1908 and 1915 their record was 59 wins and 4 ties.

In the late 1800s / early 1900s, football was a rough, dangerous sport, plagued by violence, and featuring plays and formations that frequently resulted in injuries. Annual contests, such as the Yale-Harvard game and the Army Navy game, were cancelled some years because of the bloody results.

In 1905, 19 players were killed across the United States in football games, prompting President Theodore Roosevelt to threaten to ban the sport if it was not cleaned up. Subsequently, rule changes were instituted to tame the sport.

What team uses one stadium for regular season games, and another stadium for playoff games?

The Montreal Alouettes, in their various incarnations, played all of their games since the 1970s in the cavernous Olympic Stadium. The much-loathed park was thought to actually deter fans from coming out to games, due to its sombre atmosphere.

In 1997, the Alouettes began playing regular season games at Percival Molson Memorial Stadium, on the campus of McGill University. The new venue proved to be a hit, drawing raucous, sell-out crowds, and the team made it their permanent home.

However, due to its small size (it seats a mere 20,000 fans), it is not suitable for playoff games, so the team plays at Olympic Stadium in the postseason.

> **Quickies**
>
> *Did you know ...*
>
> • That before the 1960s there was no scoreboard clock in NFL stadiums? Time was kept on the referee's wristwatch, and fans only had the two-minute warning to let them know how much time was remaining in a half.

How many incarnations of the Montreal Alouettes have there been?

Three different Montreal teams have gone by the name "Alouettes." The first, founded in 1872, adopted the name "Alouettes" (French for "lark") in 1946. This incarnation was forced to fold after the 1981 season, when team owner Nelson Skalbania — who had only purchased the team a year earlier — filed for bankruptcy as his financial empire collapsed.

The following season, Charles Bronfman revived football in Montreal with a new team, called the Concordes. In 1986, the Concordes, struggling to gain fan support, dipped into the past and renamed themselves the Alouettes. A year later, the team folded.

Finally, when the CFL's American experiment failed, the Baltimore Stallions moved to Montreal, and were immediately renamed the Alouettes.

Who founded the Montreal Concordes after the Alouettes folded?

After the brief and disastrous ownership of Nelson Skalbania led to the demise of the original Montreal Alouettes football club in 1981, it was feared that French Canada would be without a representative in the CFL.

Charles Bronfman, of the famed Bronfman family that earned its fortune as distillers, was a prominent figure on the Montreal sports scene as the owner of baseball's Expos since the team's inception. Convinced that football was still viable in the second largest city in the country, he sought, and was awarded, an expansion franchise that would take the field in 1982 — meaning that Montreal would not miss a single game of CFL action. While the team was technically considered a different franchise and bore a different name — the Concordes — they used the same facilities and had the same players as the defunct Alouettes.

Quickies
Did you know ...
• That Halifax, Nova Scotia, was granted a CFL franchise in 1984 (the Atlantic Schooners), but the team folded before ever playing a game because they couldn't finance a new stadium?

What was the most successful American team in the CFL?

The CFL's American expansion began in 1993, but the most successful franchise to play south of the border did not take the field until 1994. The Baltimore Stallions, who played out of the city's aging Memorial Stadium, burst out of the gates in their first season with a 12–6 regular season record, and then advanced to the Grey Cup, where they lost on a last-second field goal by Lui Passaglia.

In 1995, the team was even better, putting together a 15–3 record and returning to the Grey Cup, where they became the first, and last, American team to win Canada's football championship by defeating the Calgary Stampeders, 37–20. The following year, the Stallions moved to Montreal, and were the only American franchise to survive the collapse of the CFL's ambitious experiment.

City of Champions

Baltimore is the only city that has won football championships in three different leagues with four different teams.

- Baltimore Colts (Super Bowl V, 1972)
- Baltimore Stars (1985 USFL Championship)
- Baltimore Stallions (1995 Grey Cup)
- Baltimore Ravens (Super Bowl XXXV, 2002)

Who has been a CFL player, team president, and league commissioner?

While the feat seems improbable, two men have managed to participate in the CFL as player, team president, and league commissioner.

Though the modern CFL did not technically exist in his playing days, Jake Gaudaur was a member of three teams that ultimately became mainstays in the CFL: the Hamilton Tigers (later Tiger-Cats), the Toronto Argonauts, and the Montreal Alouettes. After retiring, he was president of the Tiger-Cats from 1954 to 1967, and CFL commissioner from 1968 to 1984.

Larry Smith took a somewhat different route. A player with the Montreal Alouettes from 1972 to 1980, he became league commissioner in 1992, then, after American expansion failed, he stepped down to become president of the former Baltimore franchise, which had relocated to Montreal.

What sport was the Grey Cup originally intended for?

The image of the Grey Cup has been central to Canadian football for generations. And yet, it was never intended to be a football trophy at all.

When Albert Henry George Grey, the fourth Earl Grey, decided to donate a championship trophy that would bear his name, he intended it to be awarded to the Canadian senior hockey champion. Unfortunately, while he was busy preparing his legacy, Sir Montague Allan was donating the Allan Cup for that very purpose. Earl Grey then shifted gears and decided his trophy would be awarded to the champion team from the Canadian Rugby Union (an early Canadian football association). Fortune was on Grey's side; while both trophies continue to be contested annually, the Grey Cup is, obviously, the more famous of the two.

What championship trophy was given to its first winners three months after their victory?

The first Grey Cup game was played in 1909 at Rosedale Field in Toronto. The University of Toronto team knocked off the Parkdale Canoe Club, 26–6. But if the U of T players were hoping to sip from the cup to celebrate their win, they would have been disappointed. The cup had not been made yet. The order was only placed two weeks before the game, which was not nearly enough time for the silversmiths to complete their work.

When the cup was finally ready in March 1910, at a cost of $48, it was presented to the University of Toronto. Clearly the team was not eager to give up the long-awaited prize — they won the championship the next two seasons as well.

> **Quickies**
> *Did you know ...*
> • That two teams — the Jets and the Giants — have "New York" as their city name, but neither plays in the city, or the state, of New York? Both play their games at Giants Stadium in New Jersey. Ironically, the NFL's head offices are in New York City — a city without a team.

What is the Canadian Bowl?

The Canadian Bowl is the championship of the Canadian Junior Football League, an association of amateur teams from across the country. Established in 1890, the league is open to players aged 17–22, and is intended to provide competitive opportunities for post-high school athletes. A number of players have gone on to play in the CFL, while others have played for Canadian universities. (Players are still eligible to play for Canadian Interuniversity Sports teams, as long as they play no more than two seasons in the CJFL.)

What is the only U.S. college football bowl game played outside the United States?

In 2007, the NCAA decided to add to its already enormous roster of post-season bowl games by venturing into Toronto for the International Bowl. Played at the Rogers Centre (formerly the SkyDome), the game features teams from the Big East Conference and the Mid-American Conference.

What Canadian university football team was part of U.S. college football until 2002?

The National Association of Intercollegiate Athletics differs from the NCAA in that it is an association of smaller colleges, and it allows international entries. The Simon Fraser University Clan, wanting to compete in a system that allowed full scholarships (which were not permitted in Canada at the time) joined the NAIA in 1965, and continued to play in the American system until joining the CIS in 2002.

How did the Hamilton Tiger-Cats get their hyphenated name?

The early history of football in Hamilton, Ontario, is a story of mergers. The original Hamilton Tigers co-existed with the Hamilton Alerts in the early 1900s, and won five Grey Cups between 1913 and 1932. During World War II a separate team, the Hamilton Flying Wildcats, emerged and won the 1943 Grey Cup.

But in the post-war era, the two teams found themselves in financial difficulties, due to the fact that they were competing for the same fan base. So in 1950, they merged. They combined their names into "Tiger-Cats." For some time they also combined team colours — the black and yellow of the Tigers were joined by the red, white, and blue of the Flying Wildcats. Over time, the overkill of colours was pared down to the current black, yellow, and white.

What city did the NFL Rams originally play in?

The Rams franchise broke the hearts of Los Angeles football fans in 1995, when they moved to St. Louis, leaving L.A. without an NFL team for the first time in decades. To make matters worse, the Rams went on to win the Super Bowl in 1999 — something they failed to do in their years in Los Angeles.

But long before the hearts of Californians were broken, the Rams were located in another city. The Cleveland Rams were members of the NFL beginning in 1937, and played for nine seasons before moving to Los Angeles.

What NFL teams have represented Los Angeles?

Though no teams currently play in Los Angeles, four teams have in the past. Two are easy for most fans to name: the Raiders (who moved to L.A. from Oakland, then returned to Oakland later) and the Rams (who arrived from Cleveland, and later moved to St. Louis). Other fans will recall that the San Diego Chargers began life as the Los Angeles Chargers, initially playing in L.A. itself, then playing out of Anaheim.

Few fans know that there was a fourth NFL team that represented Los Angeles. The Los Angeles Buccaneers were an NFL team in 1926. Unfortunately for L.A. football fans, the team never actually played at home. Made up primarily of alumni from the University of California and USC, the team played all their games on the road, and folded after one season.

Who are the only two charter-member teams still in the NFL?

In 1920 the brand new American Professional Football Association — later renamed the NFL — took to the field for the first time. While most of the teams in the league failed to last the entire history of the league, two charter members are still playing today. The first is recognizable because of its name: the Chicago Cardinals would later move to St. Louis, and then Phoenix. The other team was the Decatur Staleys. The Staleys moved to Chicago in 1921, and later changed their name to the Bears.

While not a charter member, the Green Bay Packers are the oldest team in the NFL that has never moved from its original home. They joined the NFL in 1921.

> **Quickies**
>
> *Did you know ...*
>
> • That in the NFL's modern era, every city that has lost a team due to franchise relocation has returned to the league, with the exception of Los Angeles? Baltimore, Cleveland, Houston, Oakland, and St. Louis have all regained NFL franchises. Los Angeles has been without a team since 1994, longer than any other former NFL city.

Why are footballs shaped the way they are?

The football used in modern times derived from the oval-shaped ball used in rugby, the game from which football evolved. A common belief is that the rugby ball became oval shaped because the original balls (before the invention of rubber) had pigs' bladders for inserts. Another belief is that the old pig's-bladder inserts with leather outer shells were prone to becoming misshapen during play, and eventually people decided to stick with the unusual shape.

None of these theories holds much water when it is considered that the soccer ball, which was also made with a pig's-bladder insert, always maintained a round shape.

In fact, the rugby ball became oval-shaped because the game required players to carry and handle the ball, and an oblong ball was far more suitable for this purpose than a large, round one.

Where did the Green Bay Packers get their name?

When the Green Bay football team was founded by Earl "Curly" Lambeau and George Calhoun, Lambeau's employer, the Indian Packing Company, donated uniforms, equipment, a practice field, and $500 in exchange for using the company's name as the team's identification. Calhoun was known to call the team the "Indian Packers" or the "Indians," and after the Indian Packing Company was bought by the Acme Packing Company, "Acme Packers" appeared on the uniforms. But the simple name "Packers" is what stuck. "Green Bay Packers" is the oldest team name still being used by an NFL team.

Who founded the AFL and why?

The American Football League was the brainchild of Lamar Hunt. Hunt, an heir to oil tycoon H.L. Hunt, sought to purchase the NFL's Chicago Cardinals and move them to Dallas in the late 1950s. Unable to do so, he approached the NFL and proposed an expansion — with himself as the owner of a new franchise. The NFL, wary of growing too quickly, turned him down.

Hunt then approached other suitors who had been turned down in their attempts to buy the Cardinals and asked them to join him in forming a new league. On August 14, 1959, six cities became charter members of the new American Football League: Dallas (Hunt's team), Houston, Minneapolis-St. Paul, Denver, Los Angeles, and New York. Later that year, Buffalo and Boston were added. The Minneapolis team never took the field — the NFL attempted to squash the new league by offering franchises to owners willing to abandon the AFL scheme. The Minneapolis owners were the only ones to accept the offer.

Hunt would later become the founding owner of the Kansas City Chiefs, and also helped to found both the North American Soccer League and Major League Soccer.

What was the Bert Bell Benefit Bowl?

The game, which was also known as the Playoff Bowl, was organized in honour of Bert Bell, the co-founder of the Philadelphia Eagles, who died at a Steelers–Eagles game in 1959. The game was played annually from 1960 to 1969, the week after the NFL Championship Game. At first, second-place teams from the NFL's Eastern and Western conferences met in the Playoff Bowl. After the NFL expanded its playoffs in 1967, the losing teams from the two semi-final matches would be designated to play in the Playoff Bowl.

Officially, the Playoff Bowl determined the NFL's overall third-place team, though the statistics are not included in official playoff statistics. The Playoff Bowl was discontinued after the AFL-NFL merger.

How long are teams allowed to hold on to the Vince Lombardi Trophy between seasons?

Unlike trophies like the Grey Cup or the Stanley Cup, there is no one Vince Lombardi Trophy. Each year, a new trophy is made and presented to the winning team at the Super Bowl. After the trophy is presented, it is sent to Tiffany & Co. (where the trophy is made) to be engraved. It is then sent back to the winning team and is theirs to keep.

Why did the Baltimore Colts receive two Vince Lombardi Trophies for winning one Super Bowl?

The rules regarding the Vince Lombardi Trophy state that it belongs to the winning team, and not the team's owner. This rankled Colts owner Carroll Rosenbloom after his team won Super Bowl V, and even more so after he traded the Colts to Bob Isray so that Rosenbloom could own the Los Angeles Rams.

Rosenbloom schemed to get the trophy from the Colts. In 1973, Los Angeles hosted the Super Bowl, and Rosenbloom told the Colts that all the Vince Lombardi Trophies to date were going to be put on display for a commissioner's banquet the weekend of the game. The Colts, trustingly, turned the hardware over to Rosenbloom. There was never a display, and he refused to return the trophy.

Commissioner Pete Rozelle, wary of getting into yet another scuffle with Rosenbloon, had another trophy made and sent to the Colts as a replacement.

What was the "Baltodome"?

In the early 1970s, the Baltimore Colts were desperate to move out of the aging Memorial Stadium, which was considered woefully inadequate as a football facility. The plan was to build a new domed stadium that was given the working name of "The Baltodome." It would be built in the Camden Yards area of Baltimore, near where baseball's Orioles would later build a stadium.

The plan seemed to be gaining steam when Maryland's legislature nixed the idea. This was followed by a successful campaign by the city's comptroller to pass measures that prohibited the building of any stadium that would replace the existing one, which was a "memorial" to veterans. Robert Isray, who had taken ownership of the Colts under the impression that a new stadium was in the works, was dismayed, and within a few years was looking at relocation options.

Who won the first time the Indianapolis Colts came back to Baltimore to play the Ravens?

After the Colts left Baltimore in a midnight move, there was a good deal of bitterness among Baltimore football fans, and much of this was directed toward the "new" Indianapolis Colts team. The bitterness did not fade over time. When Baltimore finally returned to the NFL with the arrival of the Ravens in 1996, fans eagerly awaited the first visit of the now-loathed Colts.

That first visit didn't come until November 29, 1998, but it was worth the wait. In an exciting contest, the Ravens trailed by as much as 14 points on two occasions, but with a strong second half, they outlasted the Colts for a 38–31 win.

What NFL teams merged during World War II?

Two forgotten teams of the 1940s were the Steagles and Card-Pitt.
During World War II, teams had to cut their rosters as players
were drafted to fight overseas. The Pittsburgh Steelers were down to six
players, and the Philadelphia Eagles to just over 10. In 1943, rather than
suspending operations (as the Cleveland Rams had done), the Steelers
and Eagles chose to join forces and play as one team, which the media
referred to as the "Steagles." They had a 5–4–1 record that season. The
next year, the Eagles were able to compete separately, but the Steelers
sought another merger, this time with the Chicago Cardinals. The new
team was dubbed "Card-Pitt." The Card-Pitt team didn't fare nearly as
well as the Steagles; their 1944 record was 0–10.

What NFL team has played home games in the most different stadiums without changing their geographic representation?

A number of teams have played home games in six different stadiums
without moving to a new city or region (Chicago Bears, Philadelphia
Eagles, New York Giants, Boston/New England Patriots). But one team,
the Green Bay Packers, has maintained its roots in the Milwaukee-Green
Bay area while playing in eight different stadiums.

In the early years, the Packers went through home fields quickly.
From 1919 to 1922, they played at Hagemeister Park. Next, they played
two years at Bellevue Park. In 1925, they began play at City Stadium,
where they would remain until 1956. In 1957, the Packers moved into a
facility known as New City Stadium, which was renamed Lambeau Field
in 1966 and is the team's present home.

In the meantime, for 60 years the Packers played some home games
each year in Milwaukee at Borchert Field (1933), Wisconsin State Fair
Park (1934 to 1951), Marquette Stadium (1952), and Milwaukee County
Stadium (1953 to 1994).

What NFL franchise has represented
the most different cities?

Both the Arizona Cardinals and the St. Louis Rams have done their share of travelling, representing three different cities during the course of their history.

The Cardinals began life in Chicago before moving to St. Louis in 1960. In 1988 they moved to Phoenix — their third city. (Technically, one could argue that they've represented four cities, since during World War II they temporarily merged with the Pittsburgh Steelers and played games in both Chicago and Pittsburgh.)

The Rams, meanwhile, started as the Cleveland Rams, moved to Los Angeles in 1946, and then left L.A. without a football team when they moved to St. Louis in 1995.

Another franchise, the Raiders, has made just as many city switches, but only by returning to the city in which they started. They went from Oakland, to Los Angeles, then back to Oakland.

football
in media
and popular culture

Which football players performed at Wrestlemania 2?

When the World Wrestling Federation was building its mainstream appeal in the early to mid 1980s, it did so by associating with celebrities from other industries, and celebrities were a huge part of the growth of the WWF's annual showcase, Wrestlemania.

Wrestlemania 2 was staged in three different cities, and each venue had its own main event. The main event for the Chicago show was a 20-man battle royal, which included WWF wrestlers and NFL players.

The NFL participants were: Jim Covert, Harvey Martin, Ernie Holmes, Bill Fralic, Russ Francis, and William "The Refrigerator" Perry. The NFLers did not last long, and the event was won by Andre the Giant.

Who performed on the rap record "The Super Bowl Shuffle"?

The 1985 Chicago Bears, supremely confident that they were the favourites to win the Super Bowl, released a rap record late in the regular season titled "The Super Bowl Shuffle." The single featured virtually the entire Bears team, including such household names as quarterback Jim McMahon, defensive lineman William "The Refrigerator" Perry, linebacker Mike Singletary, and halfback Walter Payton.

The only holdouts were Steve McMichael and future Hall of Famer Dan Hampton, who felt that the idea was too "cocky."

The single went to #43 on the Billboard chart, and some Bears fans accused Billboard of purposely preventing it to rise higher than that for fear that Casey Kasem would have to play the song on the weekly radio show, *America's Top Forty*.

Quickies
Did you know ...
- That the Chicago Bears' hit record "Super Bowl Shuffle" was not the first time that a team had released a single? In 1984, the San Francisco 49ers recorded the single, "We are the 49ers." Like the Bears, the 49ers won the Super Bowl in the same season that their record was released.

What football players recorded two songs with Huey Lewis and the News?

San Francisco-based Huey Lewis and the News were passionate sports fans, to the extent that they named their most successful album *Sports*. And as San Franciscans, they were naturally drawn to the hometown football team, the San Francisco 49ers.

On the album *Fore!*, the follow-up to *Sports*, the band called in some heroes: 49ers Joe Montana, Ronnie Lott, Dwight Clark, and Riki Ellison. The quartet performed background vocals on the top-10 hits "Hip to Be Square" and "I Know What I Like."

What NFL players appear in the film *Necessary Roughness*?

The Scott Bakula film *Necessary Roughness* is notable less for its cinematic brilliance, and more for the cameos by several NFL players.

Quickies

Did you know ...

• That one of Bob Marley's sons was a professional football player? Rohan Marley was a linebacker for the University of Miami, and went on to play for the Ottawa Rough Riders of the CFL.

The movie tells the story of a suspended college football program being revived — with a group of castoffs and walk-ons. Due to their low numbers, team members are forced to play on both offence and defence.

In one scene, the team plays an exhibition game against a team of convicts from a local penitentiary. Playing the roles of the convicts are NFLers Dick Butkus, Earl Campbell, Roger Craig, Ben Davidson, Tony Dorsett, Ed "Too Tall" Jones, Jim Kelly, Jerry Rice, Herschel Walker, and Randy White. Boxer Evander Holyfield is also on the prison team.

Whose scheduling conflict prevented him from playing Gale Sayers in the 1971 TV movie, *Brian's Song*?

The man who was unable to play Gale Sayers due to scheduling was Gale Sayers himself.

43

The made-for-TV movie *Brian's Song* told the story of Brian Piccolo, Sayers' teammate and fellow back on the Chicago Bears in the late sixties. Piccolo died of cancer in 1970, and Sayers, Piccolo's close friend and a featured character in the planned film, was interested in playing himself in the biopic. Unfortunately, the Bears' training schedule overlapped the shooting schedule for the film and Sayers was unable to take on the role. Instead, Louis Gosset Jr. was cast, but he also needed to be replaced when he tore his Achilles tendon while training for the film. The role was eventually played by Billy Dee Williams.

Whatever became of the real-life *Rudy*?

The 1993 film *Rudy* is the inspirational story of young man's efforts to become a member of the Notre Dame Fighting Irish football team. Despite dyslexia and a small frame unsuited to football, Rudy manages to get accepted to Notre Dame after many attempts, and is able to make the Irish's practice squad. He finally gets onto the field in the last minute of the last game for which he is eligible.

The movie is based on the real-life story of Daniel "Rudy" Ruettiger. In 1989, convinced his story would make a great film, Ruettiger met with screenwriter Angelo Pizzo, who was the writer behind another inspirational sports film, *Hoosiers*. Initially, Pizzo was uninterested, but Ruettiger persisted. Pizzo talked about the project with studio executives, and the Rudy story made another improbable journey, this time to the big screen.

Today, Ruettiger is an inspirational speaker, using his life story as an example of how determination can beat the odds.

What football player was the coveted trophy in a season of *The Bachelor*?

Canadian quarterback Jesse Palmer had brief stints with the New York Giants and San Francisco 49ers in the NFL, and the Montreal Alouettes in the CFL. But his greatest fame came when he starred in season five of the American reality show, *The Bachelor*. After narrowing down his dating options (at one point forgetting a woman's name mid-dump), Jesse settled on Jessica Bowlin. Unfortunately, as is usually the case with romance that blooms on *The Bachelor*, the relationship was short-lived and the two soon parted ways.

> **Quickies**
> *Did you know ...*
> • That only two movies have been filmed on the campus of Notre Dame University? The films are *Knute Rockne: All American* (1940) and *Rudy* (1993).

What Youngstown State University linebacker achieved lasting fame as a shoe salesman?

After graduating from YSU, Ed O'Neill was signed by the Pittsburgh Steelers and attended training camp in 1969. He was cut by the Steelers, and returned to Youngstown as a social studies teacher. He soon turned to acting, and after some theatre work he landed parts in a string of films and made-for-TV productions.

He became an icon, and hero of the common man, when he snagged the role of shoe salesman, and grudging father and husband, in the long-running sitcom, *Married ... With Children*.

What was O.J. Simpson's first major motion picture?

Throughout his playing career, O.J. Simpson moonlighted as an actor, appearing in a number of television shows. But he went Hollywood with his first major motion picture, *The Klansman*, in which he played a black man accused of raping a white woman.

From the Gridiron to the Silver Screen: Players Who have Dabbled in Acting

- Lyle Alzado
- Bubba Smith
- Don Gibb
- Lawrence Taylor
- Fred Williamson
- Terry Crews
- Brian Bosworth
- Jim Brown
- Frank McRae
- John Matuszak
- Carl Weathers
- O.J. Simpson
- Terry Bradshaw
- Mike Ditka
- Michael Irvin
- Bill Romanowski
- Brett Favre
- Alex Karras
- Bill Goldberg
- Bob Sapp
- Fred Dryer
- Howie Long
- Dwayne "The Rock" Johnson
- Dean Cain
- Burt Reynolds
- Ronald Reagan
- Mark Harmon
- Ed Marinaro
- Merlin Olsen
- Lester Speight (AKA Terry Tate: Office Linebacker)
- Mark Schlereth
- Rosey Grier
- Bob Golic
- Ed O'Neill

Simpson's acting career was marked by a number of roles in notable projects, including *Capricorn One*, the *Naked Gun* series, and the landmark television miniseries *Roots*. His last movie was *Naked Gun 33 1/3: The Final Insult*, after which his legal problems made a less-appetizing choice for casting directors.

Who was the first player ever cut by the Carolina Panthers?

Drafted in the 11th round of the 1990 draft by the Los Angeles Rams, Bill Goldberg did not seem to be destined for fame. He played for a few years in the NFL, and in 1995, when Carolina was added to the league, the Panthers drafted Goldberg and brought him to training camp. But Goldberg's Panther career never got off the ground, and he had the dubious honour of being the first player the expansion team ever cut.

But this was an era where football players often saw professional wrestling as a fallback, and Goldberg found new life in a new career. He joined World Championship Wrestling, making his debut in 1997. Over the next several years he won championships in both WCW and World Wrestling Entertainment.

What did football player Lawrence Pfohl become famous for?

As a football player, Lawrence Pfohl's career was unspectacular. He attended Penn State on a scholarship then transferred to the University of Miami, ultimately losing his scholarship there after damaging a hotel room. He then signed with the Montreal Alouettes, playing parts of three seasons from 1979 to 1981.

In 1982, Pfohl signed with the Green Bay Packers, but suffered an injury in training camp that kept him out for the entire season. The following year, the Packers cut him before the season began, and he never saw action in the NFL. In 1984 he went to the USFL as a member of the Memphis Showboats, and then the Tampa Bay Bandits.

In 1985 a career change turned Pfohl's fortunes around. He became a professional wrestler, adopted the stage name "Lex Luger," and went on to win numerous championships as a star in WCW and the WWF (now known as WWE).

Whose death was announced during a *Monday Night Football* broadcast in 1980?

On December 8, 1980, the Miami Dolphins and New England Patriots

Umm, I'm NOT with the band.
The Leland Stanford Junior University Marching Band made every sports blooper reel in North America at the end of a 1982 game when, believing the game to be over, they began to march onto the field, only to find themselves in the middle of a game-winning touchdown run by University of California, Berkley. Players had to lateral the ball to one another to avoid the tubas and drums that were in their way. This wasn't the only moment of infamy for the band, whose usual moments of infamy were intentional:

- In 1972, they mocked the kidnapping of Patty Hearst (who happened to be a student at their rival school, Cal) by forming the shape of a hamburger bun at midfield ... with no "patty."
- In 1986, one of several band members urinated on the field after a game.
- Also in 1986, the band's letter-formations at two separate games spelled out profanities.
- During a home game against visiting Notre Dame, the band performed while one member was wearing a nun's habit and using a cross as a baton.
- The band stood outside a Los Angeles courthouse during jury selection for the 1994 O.J. Simpson trial, playing the song "She's Not There" by the Zombies. (Simpson was, of course, on trial for the murder of his ex-wife.)

were in a tight battle in the final moments of regulation. Patriots kicker John Smith lined up for an attempt at a game-winning field goal (which he eventually missed, allowing the Dolphins to win in overtime). With the game on the line, veteran Monday Night Football announcer Howard Cosell broke in and told the viewers that it was just a game, then announced that John Lennon had been shot and killed in New York.

What football broadcaster was traded to another television network for a cartoon character?

In 2006, NBC was launching its Sunday Night Football program, and wanted veteran ABC/ESPN announcer Al Michaels to jump ship and join their network. ABC/ESPN's parent company, the Walt Disney Company, was willing to release Michaels from his contract so that he could join NBC, but at a price. In addition to securing the rights to expanded coverage and highlights of a number of sporting events, Walt Disney Company asked for the rights to cartoon character Oswald the Lucky Rabbit.

Oswald was a character created by Walt Disney early in his career while working for Charles Mintz and Universal Pictures. After a dispute with Mintz, Walt started his own company, but lost the rights to Oswald, who remained the property of Universal. Walt then modified Oswald by rounding his ears and renaming him "Mickey Mouse."

Universal later merged with NBC to become NBC Universal.

Quickies
Did you know ...

- That *Heaven Can Wait* was not supposed to be a football film at all? A remake of the 1941 film, *Here Comes Mr. Jordan*, director Warren Beatty wanted the lead character to be a boxer, as in the original. He had an actor in mind: Muhammad Ali. Unfortunately (or fortunately), Ali's schedule (and, perhaps, good sense) prevented that from happening. So, Beatty cast himself in the lead. Realizing he would not be plausible as a boxer, he changed the film so that the main character was a football player.

What was the "sealed bid" that commissioner Pete Rozelle demanded in 1964?

In 1964, the exclusive contract CBS had to televise NFL games came to an end. The deal had been lucrative for both sides, and the other networks knew it. So, when it came time to decide on a new deal, Pete Rozelle knew that the NFL stood to make major financial gains by opening up the bidding. Rather than having an out-and-out bidding war, he chose the "sealed bid" approach.

Each network was asked to submit a sealed manila envelope with their bid, and Rozelle opened the bids, one at a time, in front of assembled media. The first bid was from ABC, and was larger than what CBS had been paying the past two seasons. Next, he opened the NBC bid, which was even larger than the ABC bid. Finally, he opened the astonishing CBS bid, which, at $28.2 million, was several times larger than either of the previous two bids.

How many *Monday Night Football* games aired on ABC?

Monday Night Football debuted in 1970 on ABC, and remained on the network for 36 seasons — longer than any prime time network show in the United States, other than *60 Minutes.*

In 2006, the broadcast moved to ESPN. During its time as custodians of weekly tradition, ABC aired 555 *Monday Night Football* games.

Who won the first *Monday Night Football* game?

The NFL had experimented with Monday night broadcasts for several years before making it a weekly institution. The contract for *Monday Night Football* was awarded to ABC in 1970. The first game featured the Cleveland Browns defeating the New York Jets 31–21. The broadcast captured a whopping 33 percent of the TV viewing audience.

Ironically, when the Jets played in the final ABC broadcast of *Monday Night Football*, they lost to the New England Patriots by the identical score, 31–21.

What team has won the most games on *Monday Night Football*?

As of the beginning of the 2009 season, the Dallas Cowboys stand as the all-time leader in *Monday Night Football* wins with 41. On the flipside, the Chicago Bears stand as the most frequent losers of the prime time showcase with 34 losses.

When was the first football game televised?

Football made its television debut on September 30, 1939, when NBC's experimental non-commercial station, W2XBS, carried the game between Fordham University and Waynesburg College. Fordham prevailed, 34–7.

Professional football hit the airwaves for the first time three weeks later, on October 22, when the football edition of the Brooklyn Dodgers defeated the Philadelphia Eagles, 23–14.

What was the "Heidi Game"?

A highly anticipated November 17, 1968, AFL tilt saw the 7–2 New York Jets leading the 7–2 Oakland Raiders 32–29 with 1:05 remaining in the fourth quarter. Due to numerous fights and other delays, the game was running long. NBC had scheduled the premiere of a new made-for-TV adaptation of *Heidi* to air that evening at 7:00 p.m., and the game was now running into its time slot.

Certain the Jets had the game in hand — and concerned about angering the Timex watch company, who were *Heidi*'s sponsors — NBC elected to cut away from the game to show the story of the little Swiss girl.

While dumbfounded fans watched the opening scenes of *Heidi*, they missed two Raiders touchdowns that resulted in a 43–32 Oakland win.

The incident became known as "The Heidi Game," and afterwards the NFL would require that broadcasters carry games in their entirety in the markets of the competing teams.

For what it's worth, *Heidi* received positive reviews, and Joe Namath — who quarterbacked the Jets in The Heidi Game — said of the film, "I didn't get a chance to see it, but I heard it was great."

Quickies

Did you know ...

- That while filming *The Longest Yard* at Georgia State Penitentiary, Burt Reynolds made a habit of socializing with the inmates? One asked Burt where he lived. After telling him, Burt asked why the man wanted to know. The inmate answered that he'd spent his entire life burglarizing the homes of people with no money, so when he got out he wanted to rob someone with a lot of money.

What football team was named after a Burt Reynolds character?

In the early 1980s, the name "Burt Reynolds" was box office gold. So, when Reynolds became a minority owner of John Bassett's Tampa Bay entry into the new USFL, the team tried to capitalize on the star's involvement. Taking their cue from the name of one of Reynold's most famous movie franchises — the *Smokey and the Bandit* series — the team became known as the Tampa Bay Bandits.

When was the Tournament of Roses Parade first held?

Though it has come to be associated with the Rose Bowl game, the Tournament of Roses Parade actually preceded the Rose Bowl by 12 years. Pasadena's Valley Hunt Club was looking for a way to show off the mild weather they enjoyed in southern California, and paraded carriages covered with flowers through the streets. Charles Holder, a member of the club, was so taken by the sight that he suggested referring to the parade as the "Tournament of Roses."

In 1902, organizers were looking for ways to draw attention to their festival, so club president James Wagner agreed to cover the costs of bringing two top college football teams to town to play a game. Eventually, that game became the annual tradition known as the Rose Bowl.

Who has been the Grand Marshal for the Tournament of Roses Parade the most times?

As is the case with other high-profile parades, the president of the Tournament of Roses Association has traditionally invited celebrities to be the Grand Marshal. Hollywood stars such as Bob Hope and Shirley Temple, as well as Presidents Dwight Eisenhower and Richard Nixon, have been given the honour. But the most frequent Grand Marshal was Dr. Francis Rowland, whose only celebrity was being one of the founding members of the Tournament of Roses Association.

As far as people most followers will have heard of, however, Shirley Temple leads the celebrity pack, having served as Grand Marshal three times: first in 1939, and then in 1989 and 1999.

Quickies

Did you know ...

- That Burt Reynolds, who starred in the original *The Longest Yard* in 1974, was an outstanding player in real life? He played for Florida State University, and was drafted by the Baltimore Colts.

Why is the Tournament of Roses Parade sometimes held on January 2, instead of on the day of the Rose Bowl game?

Both the parade and the game were intended to take place on January 1 every year. However, early on organizers decided that they would not hold the parade on Sundays for fear of startling horses tied outside churches and disturbing the worship inside.

Few churchgoers bring their horses to service nowadays, but the obsolete rule became a tradition.

What Canadian university football team uses John Denver's "Take Me Home, Country Roads" as its theme song?

People unfamiliar with the history of the Wilfrid Laurier Golden Hawks football program are sometimes baffled that the team's theme song is the John Denver ode to West Virginia.

In the 1960s, Fred Nichols, a graduate of West Virginia's Fairmont State, came to work at Laurier and brought in three of his fellow alumni: Tuffy Knight, Rich Newbrough, and Don Smith. The team set about building a football program, with Tuffy Knight as the architect and long-time head coach. The West Virginians built one of the powerhouses of Ontario football, and saw their efforts pay off with Vanier Cup appearances in the 1970s, and eventual wins in 1991 and 2005. "Take Me Home, Country Roads" became the team's theme song in honour of the program's founders. In 2009, the walkway leading to the team's stadium in Waterloo, Ontario, was named "Country Roads Way."

Football Players and Coaches Who Have Hosted *Saturday Night Live*

- Fran Tarkenton
- O.J. Simpson
- Tom Brady
- Joe Montana
- Peyton Manning
- John Madden
- Alex Karras
- Walter Payton
- Carl Weathers
- Deion Sanders

Who did *Late Night with David Letterman* viewers choose as the subject of the "Catch Phrase for the 90s"?

David Letterman had a history of revelling in odd-sounding names, dating back at least as far as his fascination with baseball's Buddy Biancalana. He also was known for a peculiar interest in people of Swedish descent, to the point of having a camera roam the streets of New York for a recurring segment called "Let's Look for Swedes." So, when the New York Giants added Swedish-born placekicker Bjorn Nittmo to their roster in the 1989 season, Dave was in heaven.

With a new decade looming, Letterman had his audience vote for a "Catch Phrase for the 90s." The winning phrase, delivered by the kicker himself in a guest appearance, was "Who do you think you are, Bjorn Nittmo?"

Top Ten Super Bowl Commercials

10. FedEx — "Carrier Pigeons": An office worker decides to have packages delivered by carrier pigeons instead of using FedEx.

9. Pepsi — "Cindy Crawford": A couple of kids watching Cindy Crawford drink a Pepsi out of one of the newly designed cans.

8. McDonald's — "Big Mac Song": Introduced us to the jingle that simply listed the parts of a Big Mac. "Two all beef patties, special sauce, lettuce, cheese, pickles, onions on a sesame seed bun."

7. E-Trade — "Trading Baby": The first in a series of commercials intended to show that using E-Trade is so easy, even a baby can do it. A simple face-on shot of a baby working at a computer, CG lip movements making it appear the baby is speaking.

6. McDonald's — "Showdown": Larry Bird vs. Michael Jordan taking free throws from impossible locations, catching "nothing but net."

5. Reebok — "Terry Tate: Office Linebacker": Unpretentious, and pure comedy. A linebacker is hired to improve efficiency and productivity through physical and verbal intimidation. A hit ad at a time when workplace shows, such as The Office, were huge.

4. Electronic Data Systems — "Herding Cats": Few knew what the commercial was advertising, or really understood the message it was trying to deliver, but they got a kick out of watching cowboys herding cats.

3. Wendy's — "Where's the Beef?": Entirely catchphrase driven, but that catchphrase took off and became engrained in popular culture. Three elderly ladies study the "nice, big, fluffy bun" on their hamburger, while one asks, "Where's the beef?"

2. Apple — "1984": Said to be the big Super Bowl preview that started the craze of big-money, overblown ads.

1. Coca-Cola — "Mean Joe Greene": A surprisingly heartwarming ad where mean old Joe turns softie and tosses a kid his jersey after the kid gives him a Coke. The best of the bunch, because it actually produced the sentimental response it was aiming for.

What school's punishment by the NCAA inspired the film *Necessary Roughness*?

Necessary Roughness, a 1991 film starring Scott Bakula, tells the story of the fictional Texas State University Armadillos, whose football program has been penalized for corruption. They must play their season with a completely new team of coaches and players.

The film was a light take on the very serious "death penalty" imposed on Southern Methodist University in 1987. The school had already been placed on probation several times for a number of violations, including making payments to players, contrary to NCAA rules. Not only did the NCAA discover that players continued to receive payments after a 1985 penalty for the violation, but they learned that school officials had lied to them by saying the payments had stopped.

The school's entire 1987 season was cancelled, and they were only allowed to play road games in 1988. Limitations were placed on their ability to hire coaches and award scholarships. Existing players were permitted to transfer to other schools,

In 1988, SMU voluntarily cancelled a second season when they discovered that all they were left with was a team of freshmen.

> **Ten Great Football Movies**
> - *Brian's Song* (James Caan, 1971)
> - *The Longest Yard* (Burt Reynolds, 1974)
> - *Remember the Titans* (Denzel Washington, 2000)
> - *Rudy* (Sean Astin, 1993)
> - *Jerry Maguire* (Tom Cruise, 1996)
> - *Friday Night Lights* (Billy Bob Thornton, 2004)
> - *The Express* (Rob Brown, 2008)
> - *We Are Marshall* (Matthew McConaughey, 2006)
> - *Heaven Can Wait* (Warren Beatty, 1974)
> - *Lucas* (Corey Haim, 1986)

Who played Mary's ex-boyfriend in the film *There's Something About Mary*?

Packers quarterback Brett Favre made a surprise cameo appearance in the 1998 Ben Stiller and Cameron Diaz film, *There's Something About Mary*. The comedy tells the story of multiple suitors using deceit and trickery in pursuit of the Cameron Diaz character, Mary. Throughout the film Mary makes reference to an ex-boyfriend named Brett. In the closing scene, "Brett" turns out to be Brett Favre, playing himself.

But while Favre is portrayed as the perfect match for Mary, she decides she would rather be with Ben Stiller's character, saying, "I'm a Niners fan."

rules and lingo

How did the word *sack* come to be used to describe the tackle of a passer behind the line of scrimmage?

Sack only entered the football lexicon in the late sixties and early seventies — previously, the play was known as a tackle behind the line of scrimmage.

Future hall of famer Deacon Jones specialized in the tackle, but thought a shorter term was in order. He coined the word "sack," likening the devastation caused by tackling a quarterback to the sacking of a city in war. As an added bonus, according to Jones, "the word is so short you can even get 'Deacon' in front of 'Jones' in some headlines."

What little-known rule helped the Chicago Bears win a 2007 game over the Philadelphia Eagles?

Quickies
Did you know ...
That in China, the Mandarin word for American football is gan lan qui, which loosely translates to "olive ball"? The name comes from the football's shape.
In Australia, the game is called "gridiron football," while most of the rest of the world calls it "American football."

The mid-season tilt was tied 9–9 in the fourth quarter, when a penalty call *against* the Bears actually helped to save their game. A botched snap went cleanly between the legs of Bears quarterback Brian Griese, and was recovered by Eagles safety Sean Considine, who had a path to the end zone.

But the referee blew the play dead.

While a snap that goes over the head of a quarterback is a live ball, it is illegal to snap a ball between the legs of a quarterback without him touching it. The penalty for this infraction is a false start, and the ball is immediately declared dead.

No one could explain the reason that the rule is in the books, but the Bears were happy to be penalized. Rather than giving up a touchdown, they held possession and ended up with a field goal a few plays later, going on to win the game 19–16.

Why is a play referred to as a *down*?

An old rugby rule allowed a player to voluntary halt the play when held by opponents, providing the opponents agreed to the stoppage. The player would call "held," and the opponents would grant consent by responding "have it down."

Early football games allowed for a similar voluntary stoppage (without the consent of the opponent) by shouting "down." The word eventually became used to denote a play itself, and not just the completion of the play.

Though the option is rarely used, some football leagues, including the NFL, still allow for a ball carrier to voluntarily end a play by shouting, "down."

If a punter misses the ball with his kick, is the ball live? And what happens if someone hits the kicker?

According to the rules, if a punter misses the ball with his foot, it is not considered a "kick." It is considered a live ball — a fumble — and can be recovered. The opposing team is free to hit the would-be kicker without fear of a "roughing the kicker" penalty, because without a kick, there is no kicker to rough.

Quickies

Did you know ...

- That under the "fair-catch kick" provision, a team making a fair catch has the option of kicking an uncontested field goal from the spot of the catch? The opposing team must line up 10 yards downfield.

Why is a football called a *pigskin*?

Prior to the invention of vulcanized rubber in 1844, sports such as rugby and soccer needed inflatable balls for play. Animal bladders were easy to obtain and were well-suited for the purpose. In the early days of football, animal bladders were still in wide use, with pig's bladders being the choice of discerning sportsmen. The balls were known as "pigskins," presumably because players didn't want to be reminded of what part of the pig the balls came from.

By the late nineteenth century, animal bladders were replaced with rubber bladders, and the modern football contains no pig parts. The nickname, however, remains.

Why is a touchdown worth six points?

In an early form of the game, teams could only score by kicking. When a touchdown was made, it only allowed a team to kick for a point. (Points could also be scored by kicking without the benefit of a touchdown.)

In the early 1880s, it was decided that touchdowns should be more valuable than kicks from the field, and a points system was introduced. At first, a touchdown counted as four points, and the subsequent kick was worth another four points. Then, in 1897, the value of a touchdown increased to five points, while the kick after was reduced to a single point.

The touchdown became worth six points in American football in 1912. Canadian football stuck with the traditional five points until 1956, when the touchdown increased from five to six points.

Why are the lines on a football field five yards apart?

The goal in legalizing the forward pass was to reduce the number of injuries in what had become a dangerous sport. In the early days of the forward pass, rules officials tried to maximize safety by forbidding any pass made within five yards of the center. To make it easier for officials to determine whether a pass had travelled five yards, lines were painted on the field at five-yard intervals as a frame of reference.

Originally, the lines were painted both horizontally and vertically, giving the field a checkerboard pattern and leading to the sport's nickname, "gridiron." In 1910 the vertical lines were eliminated.

What quarterback had egg on his face in 2008, after admitting to not knowing a game could end in a tie?

Despite having played 10 seasons in the NFL, Philadelphia Eagles quarterback Donovan McNabb was surprised to see a 2008 game against the Cincinnati Bengals end after a single overtime period. Yet, by NFL rules, regular season games are declared ties if the teams remain deadlocked after one overtime. Playoff games continue until there is a winner.

"I've never been part of a tie," McNabb said after the game. "I never even knew that was in the rule book." McNabb had actually been in 11 regular season overtimes in his career; the previous games had resulted in ties.

People may have been more forgiving if McNabb hadn't gone on to express what he thought was a legitimate concern: "I'd hate to see what would happen in the Super Bowl and in the playoffs."

Why is a field goal worth three points?

Football started out as a kicking-oriented game, and the scoring reflected this. At

From the Rulebook: According to NCAA rules...

- Cheerleaders and bands are prohibited from making noise loud enough to prevent either team from hearing its signals.
- Players in college football are allowed to wear bandanas, but only if they're under their helmets with no part of the bandana visible.
- If a defending player leaps and knocks down a field-goal attempt as it's about to sail over the crossbar, it's a penalty, but if the defending player catches the ball, it's legal.
- If a team repeatedly commits fouls that only result in halving the distance to the goal line, the referee has the authority to award the game to their opponent.

first, the only way a team could score was by kicking. Later, when the touchdown became a point-getter of its own, a new scoring system was introduced. A field goal was worth a whopping five points, and carried more value than a touchdown.

As the touchdown became a source of excitement — and proved to be a tougher feat than a field goal — the scoring changed and in 1904 the value of a field goal was reduced to four points. Five years later, in 1909, it was devalued again to three points.

When was instant replay introduced as a means of reviewing calls in the NFL?

Although criticized by many as a dehumanizing of the game, instant replay was approved for use in the NFL in 1986. At the time, only the officials could call for an instant replay. The system suffered from a limited number of cameras — resulting in poor angles for many disputed plays — and was ultimately abandoned in 1992.

In 1999, technology, and the number of available cameras, had increased considerably and the league decided to give it another go. This time, the "coach's challenge" was introduced, allowing teams to call for reviews of up to two plays per game. (Later, a third challenge was allowed for teams that had been successful on their two previous challenges.) For several years, instant replay was only used during the regular season, but was approved for use in the playoffs beginning in 2005.

The system was considered temporary until 2007, when the NFL owners voted by an overwhelming 30–2 margin to make instant replay a permanent part of the game.

Quickies

Did you know ...

- That up until 1965, the flags thrown by NFL officials were white?
- That the 1948 Los Angeles Rams were the first NFL team to put a logo on their helmets?
- That the technical term for the shape of a football is a *prolate spheroid*?
- That in 1997 Liz Heaston became the first female to play NCAA football, with Division III school Willamette University? She kicked two extra points in the one game she played.
- That the New England Patriots were known as the Boston Patriots until 1970?

When was instant replay introduced as a means of reviewing calls in the CFL?

While instant replay had been in use off and on in the NFL since 1986, and regularly since 1999, the CFL's board of governors did not approve the officiating aid until 2006.

Where does the word *tackle* come from?

The Middle Dutch word *tacken* meant "to grab" or "to hold." The word evolved in English and by the eighteenth century *tackle* referred to harnessing equipment used on horses. The word was borrowed by early rugby to refer to the grabbing or "harnessing" of another player, and ultimately was adopted as a football term.

Notable Rule Changes in American Football

1906: Forward pass legalized
1912: Value of a touchdown increased to six points
1942: NFL requires players to wear protective headgear
1946: Free substitution forbidden, replaced by limited substitution
1948: Plastic helmets forbidden
1949: Free substitution restored
1956: Grabbing the facemask made illegal
1962: AFL makes the scoreboard clock the official clock
1967: Slingshot goal posts became the NFL standard
1974: Sudden death overtime adopted for regular-season games
     NFL goal posts moved to the back of the end zone
1980: 45-second clock replaces the 30-second clock
1994: Two-point conversion an option after touchdowns
1995: Quarterbacks permitted to receive communication from the bench via radio
     transmitters in their helmets
1999: Instant replay for the review of calls returns to the NFL on a temporary basis
2007: Instead replay for the review of calls is accepted as a permanent facet of
     the game

Why was the two-minute warning introduced?

Though the two-minute warning now exists merely as a scheduled time-out for both teams, it was originally the "warning" that the name implies.

For much of football's history, the scoreboard clock was either non-existent or unofficial, and the actual game time was kept by a referee. Because of frequent discrepancies, a two-minute warning was called by the referee so that both teams knew exactly how much time was left.

During the AFL-NFL merger, the scoreboard clock became the official clock, thus taking away the need for the "warning," but the benefits of the timeout — and the commercial revenue opportunity it provided broadcasters — had become an integral part of the game.

When did the NFL move the goal posts to the back of the end zone?

A key difference between the American and Canadian games is that in American football the goal posts are at the back of the end zone, while in Canadian football they're on the goal line.

Originally, in American football the posts were placed on the goal line, but this resulted in numerous injuries, so in 1927 they were moved to the back in both the professional and college games. In 1932 the NFL decided to move the posts back to the goal line, and they remained there until 1974. That year, the NFL moved the posts to the back of the end zone again.

Moving the posts to the back of the end zone would be more difficult for the Canadian game, which has 20-yard end zones.

Where does the term *snap* come from?

In the early days of the game, when rugby was evolving into football, the hands were not used to put a ball in play. Instead, a player put his foot on the ball and, with a snapping motion, caused it to go to his teammate. While later rule changes allowed the use of the hands to deliver the ball from the line of scrimmage to a teammate, the term "snap" remained.

Why are players' numbers determined by their position?

At one time, players were allowed to wear whatever number they wanted. But in the interest of making it easier for officials to identify eligible receivers, regulations were brought in. College and professional regulations differ somewhat, but are relatively close to the model brought in by the NFL in 1973.

What is the "Rooney Rule"?

The Rooney Rule was adopted by the NFL in 2003, and requires any team with an available head-coaching position to include at least one visible minority candidate among their interviewees.

The rule was named for Dan Rooney, owner of the Pittsburgh Steelers, who came up with the rule as chair of the NFL's diversity committee. At the time, it was felt that visible minorities, specifically African-Americans, were underrepresented among the ranks of NFL coaches.

For the most part, teams have complied, though in 2003 the Detroit Lions were fined after hiring Steve Mariucci as head coach without interviewing other candidates. The Lions argued that they had contacted minority candidates who declined to be interviewed.

You CAN Tell the Players Without a Program — NFL Positional Numbering

1–9:	Quarterbacks and kickers
10–19:	Tight ends and receivers, but only when higher numbers are unavailable
20–49:	Running backs and defensive backs
50–59:	Centres and linebackers
60–79:	Defensive and offensive linemen
80–89:	Tight ends and receivers
90–99:	Defensive linemen and linebackers

What is the "Emmitt Smith Rule"?

Critics occasionally refer to the NFL as the "No Fun League" because of its frequent rules to eliminate on-field celebrations. One such rule became known as the "Emmitt Smith Rule." The Dallas Cowboys running back was known for celebrating his touchdowns by removing his helmet. The NFL felt that this encouraged taunting and excessive celebration, and in 1997 adopted a rule forbidding players from removing their helmets on the field, except during timeouts or breaks between quarters.

What is a "rouge"?

While fans of the Canadian game rarely use the term *rouge* nowadays, the word is still used in the official rules.

A rouge is a single point that is scored when a ball is either kicked through the end zone, or kicked into the end zone and not returned past the goal line by the receiving team. This can occur on punts, missed field goal attempts, or kickoffs. A point after a touchdown is not considered a "rouge," nor is the three-point field goal.

The rouge, or single, is unique to the Canadian game. It is not clear how the word *rouge* came to be applied to the score.

Football Slang

Alligator arms — When a receiver does not extend his arms far enough to catch a ball

Blutarsky — A quarterback with a 0.0 rating in a game

Coffin corner — The corner of the playing field in front of the end zone, but next to the sidelines

Garbage time or junk time — The period at the end of a blowout, where the outcome is known, but the teams are still playing out the clock

Pooch punt — A kick purposely made short of the opposing goal line

Sidewalk alumni — Fans of a college or university team who have never actually attended that school

Taxi squad — Reserve players who are technically on a team, but never get into a game

What is the origin of the word *scrimmage*?

The word *scrimmage*, as used in North American football, evolved from the rugby term *scrummage*, which is generally shortened to *scrum* and refers to the mass of players fighting for the ball to start play.

Interestingly, though the North American term sprung from the rugby term, they both have a common origin that is, in fact, closer to the North American word. *Scrummage* comes from *scrimish*, which is an older variation of the modern word, *skirmish*.

Who supplies the balls for professional football games?

Generally, the home team is responsible for supplying footballs in most leagues. The NFL, for example, requires that home teams provide 36 balls for outdoor games, and 24 for indoor games. The balls must be given to the referee at least two hours before game time so that he can test them with a pressure gauge.

In addition, for every game, 12 new balls are shipped to the stadium, sealed in a box that can only be opened by the referee. These balls are to be used exclusively for kicking.

> **Quickies**
> **Did you know ...**
> • That the Canadian Football League rulebook requires that a *minimum* of seven balls be used during the course of a game? The referee may introduce these balls at his discretion, provided that at least seven are used.

How can a quarterback throw a legal forward pass from beyond the line of scrimmage?

Technically, he can't, but the rule is often misunderstood. Philadelphia Eagles fans found this out the hard way during the third quarter of a game against the New York Giants, in 2009.

On a third-down play in the third quarter, Giants quarterback Eli Manning, with the line of scrimmage outside the Eagles' 20-yard line, threw for an apparent first down. But the referee overturned the gain, saying that Manning was past the line of scrimmage when he released the ball, therefore it was an illegal forward pass, and the Giants would have to try for a field goal to get to within a point of the Eagles.

The Giants challenged the call. On reviewing the play, the referee noted that Manning's back foot was on the line of scrimmage when the ball was released, and according to the rule if ANY part of the passer's body is on or behind the line of scrimmage, the pass is legal.

The Giants were awarded a first down, scored a touchdown, and went on to win the game, 36–31.

strategy and plays

Who first decided to pick up the ball and carry or throw it?

According to one legend, a student at the British Public School of Rugby named William Webb Ellis was playing a kicking game, and decided to pick up the ball and run with it. In doing so, he invented a new sport, called *rugby*. Much doubt has been cast on this legend, but many still treat the story with reverence.

As rugby evolved into the modern game of football, many variations of the North American sport existed, and in 1874, versions of "football" varied greatly. That year, Montreal's McGill University football team was invited to visit Harvard in the United States for a match against their squad. On arrival, it was discovered that the two teams were playing very different brands of "football." The version played by McGill University was a form of rugby, and involved carrying the ball and throwing it. The Harvard version was a kicking game closer to soccer.

The teams solved the problem by playing two games — one under each school's rules. The Harvard team was so excited by the McGill version of the game that they adopted the new rules, and this variety of football spread rapidly in the United States, ultimately becoming a base on which the modern game was built.

Offensive Formations #1

The announcers talk about what kind of formation is being used, but many football fans don't know the difference between one formation and another. The following is a handy guide to the basic formations.

Pro Set: Two wide receivers, two running backs, one tight end. The quarterback is behind the centre, close in so that the snap is a hand-off rather than a throw, and the backs are behind the quarterback, one on either side.

Who created the Statue of Liberty play?

One of the more famous, but rarely used, trick plays in football is the Statue of Liberty play. In the simplest and most common version of the play, the quarterback rolls back, and moves his throwing hand in position to pass, but retains the ball in his non-throwing hand, and holds it behind his back. Then a receiver, or back, takes the ball and runs in a direction opposite to where the quarterback is apparently throwing.

At the point of the fake, the positioning of the quarterback's arms are similar to the pose of the Statue of Liberty, giving the play its name.

The play was invented by the Grand Old Man of College Football, Amos Alonzo Stagg. The legendary coach and pioneer of the game was not responsible for its popularity, though — credit for the play's spread goes to University of Michigan coach Fielding Yost.

> **Defensive Formations #1**
> 4–3 defence: Four down linemen on the line of scrimmage (two defensive ends on the outside, with two defensive tackles in the middle), and three linebackers behind them. Positioning of the two cornerbacks and two safeties depends on the kind type of pass coverage they are in.

Why is Canadian football considered a "passing" game while American football is considered a "running" game?

The rules and the size of the playing field have made the Canadian game a haven for the quarterback who loves big passing plays.

With only three downs to work with, short yardage gains put Canadian teams in down trouble, meaning that the grind-it-out tactic often employed by American teams to gain a few yards at a time on the ground is risky.

Also, the Canadian field is much larger than the American field. It's longer, 110 yards from goal line to goal line, with 20-yard endzones, making it a total of 30 yards longer than the American field. It's also wider, measuring 65 yards from sideline to sideline, compared to the 53 1/3-yard width of American fields. With so much more room, passing plays are more difficult to defend against.

When was the two-point conversion introduced?

In 1958 the NCAA adopted its first new scoring rule in 46 years with the introduction of the two-point conversion. Teams made good use of it on the first weekend, with five games turning on the success or failure of two-point converts.

The AFL followed suit in 1960, but the NFL was slow to warm up to the rule, and when the two leagues completed their merger in 1970, the rule was snuffed out. Eventually, the NFL came to see merit in the rule, and adopted it in 1994.

How often are two-point conversions successful?

The success rate of two-point conversions has varied wildly over the years. In the early days of the rule's existence it was estimated that two-point attempts were successful only 35 percent of the time.

By the time the NFL adopted the rule in 1994, success rates had improved; estimates generally place the success rate for both the NFL and NCAA around 43 percent. For comparison, one-point attempts are successful around 98 percent of the time.

Who scored the first two-point conversion in the NFL?

The two-point conversion scored in a regular-season NFL game actually occurred on a trick play. On the opening weekend of the 1994 season, in a game between the Cleveland Browns and the Cincinnati Bengals, Browns punter Tom Tupa was acting as the placeholder on an extra-point attempt. After taking the snap, he took the ball into the end zone himself for the two-point score. The play earned Tupa the nickname "Two-Point Tupa."

Where does the shotgun formation get its name?

The term *shotgun formation* became popular when the San Francisco 49ers made heavy use of the formation in the 1960s. The formation spreads receivers widely, and the scattering of these receivers is likened to the scattering of a shotgun blast.

Offensive Formations #3
Single set back: A formation with many variations, the single set back puts the quarterback directly behind the centre, and one running back behind him.

Who created the Run and Shoot offence?

While credit is often given to long-time coach and offensive coordinator Darell "Mouse" Davis, the Run and Shoot was actually invented by Glenn "Tiger" Ellison, a high school football coach who developed the offence for his teams, and published a book about the strategy called *Run and Shoot Football: Offense of the Future* in 1965.

The basic Run and Shoot offence uses four receivers, one running back, a quarterback, and five linemen. The receivers run short and medium routes in a passing-centric offence, while spreading out the defence to create running lanes.

Mouse Davis took to the strategy, and employed it as a coach with Portland State University. He later brought the offence to professional football, first with the Toronto Argonauts (who won a Grey Cup using the Run and Shoot after Davis's departure) and then the USFL's Houston Gamblers.

The Run and Shoot gained some popularity in the NFL in the late 1980s and early 1990s, most notably with Warren Moon and the Houston Oilers, but is seldom used at the professional level today.

Defensive Formations #3
4–4 defence: Four down linemen and four linebackers. This defence goes with only three defensive backs, removing one safety from the field.

When was the term "Hail Mary pass" first used?

In the 1975 Wildcard game against the Minnesota Vikings, the Dallas Cowboys found themselves at midfield with 24 seconds remaining, trailing 14–10. Needing a touchdown, quarterback Roger Staubach took the snap and rolled back to his own 40-yard line. "I closed my eyes," Staubach said after the game, "and said a 'Hail Mary' prayer." He then hurled the ball 55 yards to Drew Pearson, who caught it at the five-yard line and took it to the end zone for a touchdown.

The media took Staubach's "Hail Mary" description and began applying it to any last-ditch, desperation pass.

> **Offensive Formations #4**
> I formation: The quarterback is directly behind the centre, a fullback is behind the quarterback, and a running back behind him. There might be a tight end at one side of the line, and a wide receiver on either side.

What is an "Alley Oop"?

The "Alley Oop" in football was a more formalized version of (and a predecessor to) the Hail Mary pass.

While a Hail Mary pass is generally a chaotic, last second desperation pass, the Alley Oop was a coordinated, practiced play employed by the San Francisco 49ers in the 1950s. Wide receiver R.C. Owens, who was often considerably taller than the defensive backs guarding him, would run to the back of the end zone and quarterback Y.A. Tittle would through a high, arching pass. Owens would leap to a ball beyond the reach of the defenders and haul it in for a touchdown.

> **Defensive Formations #4**
> 5-2 defence: Five linebackers and two down linemen. On the line of scrimmage there are two defensive ends, one on either side of the defensive line, and three tackles in the middle. This defence uses a full backfield of two cornerbacks and two safeties.

While the use of the term "Alley Oop" is uncommon in football today, the term was adopted in basketball in the 1960s, and is a common play in that sport.

How often are onside kicks successfully recovered by the kicking team?

The onside kick is a high-risk strategy used by kicking teams to attempt to retain control of the ball. The best rate of success comes with catching the opposing team by surprise, but even then, the risk is high. Only 20 percent of onside kicks are successfully recovered by the kicking team.

Take away the element of surprise and the odds are even longer. Late in the game, when a team is attempting to catch up and can't afford to let the other team have the ball, an onside kick is often a necessity, and the opposition knows it. When the onside kick is anticipated, the success rate drops to between 12 and 14 percent.

What is a "West Coast Offence"?

"West Coast Offence" is a name given to the style of offence developed and perfected by Bill Walsh, first as offensive coordinator with the Cincinnati Bengals, and then, to great success, as head coach of the San Francisco 49ers.

The West Coast Offence is a pass-oriented offence. The bulk of plays in the West Coast Offence are short, horizontal passes, and the frequency of these plays forces the defence to defend accordingly. With the defence stretched out, running and passing lanes are opened up, creating holes for the running backs and opportunities for longer passes.

Unlike other pass-oriented offences, the West Coast Offence generally employs two or more running backs.

Ironically, the term "West Coast Offence" was first used with disdain. After his New York Giants defeated the 49ers in the 1985 playoffs, coach Bill Parcels scoffed at the strategy in a post-game scrum, saying, "What do you think of that West Coast Offence now?"

Offensive Formations #5
Wishbone formation: One wide receiver, one tight end, two halfbacks, and one fullback who lines up behind the quarterback. The quarterback is right behind the centre. Used primarily for running, the Wishbone allows the quarterback to run an option on either side of the line, and is suited for a triple option.

What was "R2P2"?

"R2P2" was a derisive nickname given to the offensive strategy employed by Marty Schottenheimer. Also called "Marty Ball," Schottenheimer's strategy is an ultra-conservative running game.

Schottenheimer had his teams run on first down, run on second down, pass on third down, and punt or kick a field goal on fourth down. Two R's, two P's — hence the nickname.

The approach earned Schottenheimer a great deal of success in the regular season as he amassed a career record of 200–126–1. Playoff success was hard to come by, though, as his teams combined for a 5–13 record over the course of his career, never reaching the Super Bowl.

> **Defensive Formations #5**
> Nickel defence: Four down linemen, two linebackers, and five defensive backs. Two defensive ends line up on the line of scrimmage, one at either end, with two defensive tackles in between. Two linebackers are behind this line. There are two safeties, two cornerbacks, and one nickelback. The backs are lined up to cover the wide receivers in a three-receiver offensive set. This formation is designed to defend against the pass.

Where did the "Wildcat formation" get its name?

The Wildcat formation is one that has gained popularity in recent years. It's most notable feature is that the quarterback does not line up behind the centre. Instead, a running back sets up behind the centre and takes the snap.

There are competing claims to the origins of the formation, both stemming from teams named the "Wildcats." One credits Hugh Wyatt, coach of the La Center High School Wildcats, who published an article that detailed the formation in *Scholastic Coach* magazine. The other major claim points to Steve Bush, who is currently an assistant coach with the Miami Dolphins, but supposedly developed the formation while coaching the West Genesee High School Wildcats.

Whatever the origins, most NFL teams have now begun using variations of the Wildcat formation. Meanwhile, the CFL, specifically seeking to allow the formation, revised their longstanding rule that required the quarterback to be in position to take the snap.

How are American/Canadian football and rugby league similar?

Rugby league differs from rugby union in a number of ways, but has a number of similarities with the North American game of football. Famed rugby league coach Jack Gibson described the relationship of rugby league and North American football as "Same game, different rules."

Both are played on gridiron-style fields, North American football measured in yards (and marked off every 10 yards) and rugby league measured in metres (marked every 10 metres). Both sports give the team on offence a number of plays, though in North American football, teams can get a new set of downs by travelling 10 yards, while in rugby league teams get a set of six tackles, with no way of getting a "first down" again. They must score or give up the ball after six plays.

Both games begin plays with a scrimmage, rather than the typical rugby scrum. Both games can advance the ball by running it, though only football allows forward passes, while rugby league teams frequently advance the ball by kicking and recovering it. Meanwhile, rugby league players play on both offence and defence.

The two games are, indeed, very different, but the number of similarities prove them to be close cousins.

What is the "flying wedge"?

The flying wedge was easily the most controversial formation in the history of football. Introduced by Harvard in 1892, the flying wedge as a dangerous manoeuvre that called for offensive players to link arms and form a V-shaped wedge with the ball carrier tucked behind them, and drive the point of the V toward the defence to move the ball carrier forward. The wedge was difficult to penetrate, and defenders found that the "best" way to defend against the formation was to throw themselves at the legs of the rushing players.

It was extraordinarily dangerous, and resulted in many injuries. After President Theodore Roosevelt threatened to ban the sport if violence

Defensive Formations #6

Dime defence: The primary feature of this formation is the use of six defensive backs: two safeties, two cornerbacks, a nickelback, and a dimeback. Up front there may be either four down linemen and one linebacker, or three down linemen and two linebackers. This formation is designed to defend against the pass.

was not eliminated, the Intercollegiate Athletic Association of the United States (which later became the NCAA) made a number of rule changes, including banning mass-momentum plays such as the flying wedge.

Police riot squads now use a manoeuvre called the flying wedge — similar to the football play — to break up unruly mobs.

legends, characters, and heroes

Who was the only NFL player to rush for more than 2,000 yards in a fourteen-game season?

As a member of the 1973 Buffalo Bills, O.J. Simpson barely eclipsed the mark, rushing for 2,003 yards on the season. Five years later, the NFL season expanded to 16 games, leaving O.J. Simpson as the only player to surpass the plateau in the 14-game format.

Though he has dropped well down the list over the years, Simpson ended his career after the 1979 season in second place on the all-time rushing list, with 11,236 career yards.

Why is the Pro Football Hall of Fame in Canton, Ohio?

According to the Pro Football Hall of Fame, Canton was selected as the home for the NFL's shrine for three reasons. First, it was in Canton that the American Professional Football Association — now known as the NFL — was founded. Second, Canton was the home of one of the first great football teams, the Canton Bulldogs, who featured the likes of Jim Thorpe. Third, the citizens of Canton organized a feverish campaign to become home to the Hall in the early 1960s.

Who was the first drafted player to go on to a Hall of Fame career in the NFL?

In the early years of the NFL Draft, busts were common, as were players simply electing not to go into professional football. So, with the number six pick in the first-ever NFL Draft in 1936, the Chicago Bears lucked out in drafting Joe Stydahar. The offensive tackle out of West Virginia University played with the Bears from 1936 to 1942. After serving in World War II, from 1945 to 1946, he was a four-time all-star and helped the Bears to win NFL Championships in 1940, 1941, and 1946.

Number six seems to have been a lucky number in the early years of the draft. The following season, the Washington Redskins used the number six slot to draft Sammy Baugh, the first drafted quarterback elected to the Hall of Fame.

Who was the only quarterback to start and win a college National Championship and start and win a Super Bowl?

In 1977, Joe Montana was third on the Notre Dame Fighting Irish's depth chart at quarterback, until injuries led to his insertion in the fourth quarter of a game against Purdue. Montana sparked a come-from-behind win, and was named the starting quarterback for the rest of the season. The team won all nine remaining games, then capped the season with a victory in the Cotton Bowl. Notre Dame was subsequently named National Champions.

Five years later, as a member of the San Francisco 49ers, Montana's last-quarter heroics landed his team in the 1983 Super Bowl, where they defeated the Cincinnati Bengals, 26–21. Montana was named Super Bowl MVP, and became the first quarterback to start and win a college National Championship and a Super Bowl.

What football legend played in the first ever public game of basketball?

Amos Alonzo Stagg was known as the "Grand Old Man" of college football, and helped to grow the sport as a coach, primarily at the University of Chicago (he coached his teams to a 242–112–27 record). He introduced a number of innovations to the sport, most notably the lateral, the man in motion, and the Statue of Liberty play.

Though known primarily for his contributions to football, Stagg coached other sports, such as baseball (for which he invented the batting cage), track and field (he coached the U.S. track and field team at the

1924 Olympics), and basketball. In fact, he was part of the development of basketball, having attended the YMCA Training School in Springfield, Massachusetts, with that sport's inventor, James Naismith. In March 1892, three months after Naismith invented the sport and had students play it, the first public game of basketball was played, and Stagg was a participant. Stagg's most lasting contribution to basketball was deciding that it should be played five-on-five.

What playoff hero once dated a Miss Universe winner?

Dwight Clark is best known to football fans as the player who made one of the most famous catches in history to win the 1982 NFC Championship and put the San Francisco 49ers in the Super Bowl. But as a student on campus at Clemson University, he may have been a hero to his male friends for other reasons. Clark was dating Shawn Weatherly, who was Miss USA in 1980, and Clark was with her when she went on to win the Miss Universe crown.

Quickies
Did you know ...
- That Patriots quarterback Tom Brady attended the 1982 NFC Championship Game in which Dwight Clark made the play known as "The Catch"?

What action by NFL commissioner Pete Rozelle caused Joe Namath to announce his retirement?

In the summer of 1969, only months after Joe Namath and the New York Jets upset the Baltimore Colts in Super Bowl III, commissioner Pete Rozelle took exception to Namath's part-ownership of a nightclub, Bachelors III. The club was frequented by what Rozelle called "undesirables," including co-owners with ties to gamblers. Rozelle ordered Namath to sell his interest in the club or face suspension.

Namath then stunned everyone by announcing his retirement. However, after negotiations with Rozelle, Namath eventually agreed to sell the club and returned to football less than a month into his "retirement."

Who is the Canadian Football League's pass king?

On October 28, 2000, Damon Allen of the B.C. Lions made a 45-yard touchdown pass to Alfred Jackson that moved him past the legendary Russ Jackson into sole possession of first place in the CFL's all-time passing yards list. Allen went on to become the most prolific passer in professional football history.

Who helped the Chicago Bears to win their last championship in the old National Football League, and their first Super Bowl?

"Iron" Mike Ditka was beloved by Bears fans as a coach partly because of his aggressive style and passion for the game, but also because of his long association with the Bears. Ditka was a tight end in the sixties and played on the Bears team that won the 1963 NFL Championship. When the Bears were in the market for a new head coach in 1982, team founder, owner, and former head coach George Halas targeted Ditka, who, at the time, was an assistant with the Dallas Cowboys. Ditka took over the Bears, and three years later led them to victory in Super Bowl XX.

Who did *Sports Illustrated* name the number one clutch quarterback of all time in 2006?

Saying he was "at his best in the national spotlight," *Sports Illustrated* put Joe Montana at the top of their list of all-time clutch quarterbacks in 2006.

Montana had a knack of helping his teams to win big games, dating back to his college years with the Notre Dame Fighting Irish, where a touchdown with two seconds remaining lifted the Irish to a win in the 1979 Cotton Bowl. As the heart of the San Francisco 49ers, Montana led his team to a 4–0 record in Super Bowls, and won the Super Bowl MVP three times.

What team has the most inductees in the Pro Football Hall of Fame?

With representation from such legends as George Halas, Red Grange, Dick Butkus, and Walter Payton, the Chicago Bears have had the most players and executives elected to the Pro Football Hall of Fame, with 26. Their nearest competitors are the Green Bay Packers, who boast 21 hall of famers.

Who is the only player elected to both the Pro Football Hall of Fame and the Canadian Football Hall of Fame?

Many players have had success in both the NFL and CFL, but none have been as accomplished in both leagues as Warren Moon.

After a solid college career, Moon went undrafted by the NFL, and had to look north of the border for work. He joined the Edmonton Eskimos and quickly became one of the most dominant players in league history, leading his team to five consecutive Grey Cup wins between 1978 and 1982.

Moon then converted his CFL success into NFL interest and signed with the Houston Oilers. While Moon never made it to the Super Bowl, he became one of only two quarterbacks to pass for more than 4,000 yards in consecutive seasons, and was named to the Pro Bowl nine times.

When he retired, his combined totals in the CFL and NFL established several professional football records, including most career passing yards, and most career passing touchdowns. He was elected to the Canadian Football Hall of Fame in 2001, and the Pro Football Hall of Fame in 2006.

What non-player is in both the Pro Football Hall of Fame and the Canadian Football Hall of Fame?

Bud Grant was a fantastic athlete in his own right, having played both professional basketball with the Minneapolis Lakers, and football with the Philadelphia Eagles and Winnipeg Blue Bombers. It was as a coach, however, that he became a legend.

He was named head coach of the Blue Bombers in 1957, and over the course of 10 seasons led Winnipeg to four Grey Cup wins in six appearances. In 1967 he was hired by the Minnesota Vikings, and became known as a stern disciplinarian, banning heaters from the sidelines in cold weather, and having national anthem practice to ensure that his players knew how to stand properly at attention.

Grant coached his Vikings to 11 division championships and became the first coach to lead a team to four Super Bowls, though Minnesota's famed "Purple People Eaters" were not enough to reign in the Vince Lombardi Trophy.

Grant retired in 1983. That year, he was elected to the Canadian Football Hall of Fame; in 1994, he joined the Professional Football Hall of Fame.

Who has appeared in the most Pro Bowls?

Two players are tied with the most number of Pro Bowl appearances at 14: Merlin Olsen and Bruce Matthews.

Olsen, a defensive tackle, spent his entire career with the Los Angeles Rams. He was first named to the Pro Bowl in his rookie season (1962) and continued to be selected to play in the game for 14 consecutive years, only missing out in his final year as a player, 1976.

Matthews, an offensive lineman who played as a guard and a centre, began his career in 1983 and received his first Pro Bowl selection in 1988. He played in the game every year for the rest of his career, retiring in 2001.

What two legendary coaches squared off in the 1925 Rose Bowl?

The game itself was not memorable — Notre Dame defeated Stanford 27–10, with three Irish touchdowns coming as a result of turnovers. But there were some firsts in the game: it was the first time Notre Dame played in a bowl game (the second time for Stanford), and it was the first time that Knute Rockne and Pop Warner faced one another.

Quickies

Did you know ...

- That over the course of his career (1949 to1975), George "The Fossil" Blanda became the only player to play in four different decades, play a record 26 seasons, and finish his career as the oldest person (48 years, 109 days) to play in an NFL game?

Rockne was the legendary head coach of Notre Dame from 1918 to 1930, before passing away in early 1931. Warner coached for 44 years, winning 337 games with Georgia, Cornell, Carlisle, Pittsburgh, Stanford, Temple, and Iowa State. Among his contributions to the game were the screen pass, and the use of shoulder and thigh pads for protection.

Who was known as "The Little General"?

Though he was only 5'5", Ron Lancaster became a Canadian football legend. Known for his leadership and play-calling abilities, he earned the nickname "The Little General."

Lancaster spent the first three years of his CFL career with the Ottawa Rough Riders before being traded to the Saskatchewan Roughriders before the 1963 season. He spent 16 seasons with Saskatchewan, leading them to five Grey Cup appearances, including one win.

After his playing career, Lancaster built on his "Little General" reputation as a head coach, winning Grey Cups in Edmonton and Hamilton.

What two players split quarterbacking duties for the Ottawa Rough Riders in the early 1960s?

The Ottawa Rough Riders had an eye for quarterbacking talent in the late 1950s and early 1960s. Though they originally signed Russ Jackson as a defensive back, they quickly converted him to quarterback, a position at which he became one of the all-time CFL greats.

But Jackson wasn't the only example of hidden talent discovered by the Riders. After NFL scouts had taken a pass on Ron Lancaster due to his small size, the Riders drafted him as a backup for Jackson.

Though Lancaster's Ottawa career was unspectacular, playing as he was in the shadow of Jackson, he emerged as a legend when traded to Saskatchewan. Both Russ Jackson and Ron Lancaster went on to become members of the Canadian Football Hall of Fame.

Who passed up an opportunity to interview for a Rhodes Scholarship in order to play in the CFL?

An all-around athlete, excelling in multiple sports, McMaster University's Russ Jackson was also a gifted academic. In 1958 he was his school's nominee for a Rhodes Scholarship.

However, Jackson felt the pull of professional football, and declined to interview for the scholarship, electing instead to sign with the Ottawa Rough Riders.

What was the "Steel Curtain"?

The Pittsburgh Steelers of the 1970s were one of the most dominant teams in NFL history, winning four Super Bowls. A large part of their success was due to their phenomenal defensive line. Led by the impeccable foursome of "Mean" Joe Greene, L.C. Greenwood, Ernie Holmes, and Dwight White, the Steelers defence stopped opposing offences in their tracks. In 1976 they went a stretch of nine games without allowing a touchdown.

The name "Steel Curtain" was the result of a contest. A Pittsburgh radio station challenged fans to come up with a name for the team's defence. A number of people submitted the name "Steel Curtain," which was a variation on the term "Iron Curtain" that was used to describe the line between eastern and western Europe during the Cold War era.

Whose injury caused him to lose his Oklahoma starting quarterback job to Jamelle Holieway?

Jamelle Holieway's later career was plagued by injuries, and he had only modest success at the professional level (NFL and CFL), but he made a tremendous impact during his 1985 freshman year with the Oklahoma Sooners, helping the team to an 11–1–0 record. After a victory in the Orange Bowl that season, Holieway became the only freshman quarterback to win a National Championship.

Holieway was not expected to be the starting quarterback that season. He got his opportunity after a game on October 19, in which Jerome Brown sacked the Sooners' early-season starter, Troy Aikman, breaking his ankle and ending his season.

Holieway took over the starting job. Upon returning, Aikman realized he needed to find a new school in order to be a starter again and transferred to UCLA.

Whose family encouraged him to quit football after getting cut by his fifth professional team?

Jack Kemp's early years as a pro football player were a struggle. A 17th-round draft pick, he was cut by the Detroit Lions before the 1957 season, and saw limited action with the Pittsburgh Steelers, San Francisco 49ers, and New York Giants in 1957 and 1958. He then played a single game with the Calgary Stampeders in 1959, which made him ineligible to play in the NFL that season. That may have been all right with Jack, except that the Stampeders became the fifth pro team to cut him.

In 1960, Kemp found work with the Los Angeles Chargers of the AFL, and guided the team to a 10–4 record and an appearance in the AFL Championship Game. After two seasons with the Chargers, he joined the Buffalo Bills, where he remained for eight seasons. Over the course of his AFL career, Kemp was named to seven all-star teams, and is a member of the Bills Wall of Fame.

In his post-football life, he was a member of the U.S. House of Representatives, and was the running-mate of Bob Dole in the 1996 Presidential Election.

Quickies

Did you know ...

That the Pittsburgh Steelers won Terry Bradshaw in a coin toss? The Steelers and the Chicago Bears finished the 1969 regular season with identical 1–13 records. In those days, when teams had matching records going into the NFL Draft, the tie was broken by a simple flip of a coin. The Steelers won the toss and drafted Bradshaw, who went on to a Hall of Fame career and led the Steelers to four Super Bowl wins.

Who was the last "ironman" player in the NFL — playing both offence and defence for an entire game?

There was a time when teams didn't need to bring their offences on the field to replace them with their defences, because the offences and the defences were made up of the same players. By the late 1950s, free substitution was legal at the professional level, and the old one-platoon system was primarily only seen in the college ranks.

Charles Bednarik was among the few who continued to play both ways, as a defensive linebacker and as an offensive centre.

By 1960, Bednarik's aging body had taken a beating, and he was primarily a centre. But in the fifth game of the season, his Philadelphia Eagles teammate Bob Pellegrini had to be carried off the field, and coach Buck Shaw needed a linebacker. He looked to Bednarik, who returned to ironman duty.

In that year's NFL Championship Game, Bednarik played 58 minutes. He was only on the sideline for kickoff returns.

Other players have taken turns on both offence and defence since, but no one has made it a full-time gig over the course of an entire game, let alone a season.

Who extended his middle finger for a cover photo on an issue of *Sports Illustrated*?

An August 1972 issue of *Sports Illustrated* ran a feature on Larry Csonka and Jim Kiick. The two were members of the stellar Miami Dolphins team that was favoured by many to win the Super Bowl, and, in fact, did, completing a perfect season. But the issue that ran prior to the '72 season created a furor that the Dolphins weren't expecting. Csonka is seated, his hand on his ankle, with his middle finger slyly extended. Somehow the obscene gestured was missed by the photographer and staff at the magazine, but not by the public, who were divided between the amused and the outraged.

The Not-So-Magnificent Seven: Prominent NFL Players who have been in Prison

- Michael Vick (dog-fighting and related offences)
- O.J. Simpson (armed robbery)
- Mercury Morris (drug trafficking — conviction later overturned and Morris pleaded no-contest on lesser charges)
- Dexter Manley (cocaine possession)
- Nate Newton (drug trafficking)
- Travis Henry (conspiracy to commit drug trafficking)
- Rae Carruth (conspiracy to commit murder)

What coach was attending an Army-Navy game while his team was being upset in 1926?

In 1926, the Notre Dame Fighting Irish were in a position to win a National Championship. They had a game coming up against Pittsburgh's Carnegie Tech. The Irish had demolished Carnegie Tech in each of their meetings over the past four years. So, when Coach Knute Rockne's agent asked him to attend the Army-Navy game that day to write an article for syndication, Rockne agreed, and said, "The game in Pittsburgh will not be important enough. I can put it in charge of someone else."

Taking Rockne's absence as an insult, Carnegie Tech upset the heavily favoured Notre Dame squad, 19–0.

Who were the Four Horsemen of Notre Dame?

During their sophomore seasons, Knute Rockne assembled a quartet of offensive players who would go down in football history. Jim Crowley (left halfback), Elmer Layden (fullback), Don Miller (right halfback), and Harry Stuhldreher (quarterback) joined forces in the 1924 college football season, and in their third game upset the favoured Army team, 13–4.

In his report on the game, *New York Tribune* writer Grantland Rice wrote, "Outlined against the blue-gray October sky, the Four Horsemen rode again." The name caught on, and the foursome continued to build on their reputation as they marched to a 10–0 season, and a convincing 27–10 win over Stanford in the Rose Bowl.

What was "The Greatest Show on Turf"?

"The Greatest Show on Turf" was the nickname given to the offence of the St. Louis Rams from 1999 to 2001. The passing-heavy offence was designed by offensive coordinator Mike Martz, who made good use of a quintet of outstanding players: quarterback Kurt Warner, running back Marshall Faulk, and receivers Isaac Bruce, Torry Holt, Az-Zahir Hakim, and Ricky Proehl.

In 2000 alone, the offence racked up an NFL record 7,335 yards — 5,492 by way of passing.

Ironically, despite their dominant offence, the Rams of the era are best known for the defensive play that won the 2000 Super Bowl, when Mike Jones tackled Tennessee's Kevin Dyson on the one-yard game on the last play of the game.

Whose memory is being honoured by a bridge being constructed near the Hoover Dam?

Great Football Nicknames
George "The Fossil" Blanda
Andre "Bad Moon" Rison
Ed "Too Tall" Jones
Billy "White Shoes" Johnson
William "The Refrigerator" Perry
Walter "Sweetness" Payton
"Mean" Joe Greene
"He Hate Me" (Rod Smart)
"The Minister of Defence" (Reggie White)
"Broadway Joe" Namath
Craig "Ironhead" Heyward
"The Galloping Ghost" (Red Grange)

A new bridge on U.S. Route 93, crossing the Colorado River and linking Arizona and Nevada, is set to open in 2010. The bridge has been named the Mike O'Callaghan-Pat Tillman Memorial Bridge. O'Callaghan was the former governor of Nevada, and Tillman was an All-Pro safety with the Arizona Cardinals.

In 2004, Tillman became only the second active professional football player to be killed in military combat when he lost his life in Afghanistan. Sadly, the death prompted outrage from his family, who accused military officials of covering up the fact that Tillman died as a result of friendly fire.

Who blamed his fatal illness on steroid use?

In the early 1990s, former Broncos, Browns, and Raiders defensive end Lyle Alzado was diagnosed with brain cancer. In a move that surprised most observers, Alzado publicly confessed to years of steroid abuse and blamed them for his illness. Steroids have been blamed for a number of serious illnesses, but, as Alzado's own physicians told him, brain cancer is not believed to be among them. Nevertheless, his passionate confession was taken as a warning against the dangers of steroid use.

Whose Super Bowl ring is a size 25?

William "The Refrigerator" Perry didn't set a lot of records in his solid NFL career, but one record he did set was for the largest Super Bowl ring ever produced: a massive size 25.

Better known for his size than his playing abilities, the 6'2", 382-pound Perry was a first-round draft pick of the Chicago Bears in 1985. His nickname was a reference to both his size and his prowess at the dinner table. Primarily a defensive lineman, he was occasionally used as a fullback on offence to block for Walter Payton, and even scored a touchdown in the 1986 Super Bowl — his first and only win as a player.

What two quarterbacks squared off in the 1973 Gator Bowl?

The 1973 Gator Bowl between Texas Tech and Tennessee was not a particularly noteworthy game at the time. It was a major bowl game, but neither team had a real shot at the National Championship.

The game became noteworthy because of the competing quarterbacks: Joe Barnes led his Texas Tech team to a 28–19 victory over a Tennessee team driven by Q.B. Condredge Holloway. A decade later, Holloway was the starting quarterback for the Toronto Argonauts, and Barnes was his backup. In the 1983 Grey Cup, Holloway struggled in the first half due to the effects of the flu, and was replaced in the second half with his team trailing the B.C. Lions 17-7. As the defence held the Lions at bay, Barnes plugged away and, with 2:44 remaining and down by five, tossed a touchdown pass to Cedric Minter for an 18–17 Toronto victory.

Who declared "It will take an act of God to beat us on Saturday" prior to a 1969 CFL playoff game?

The Toronto Argonauts faced the Ottawa Rough Riders in the two-game total-points Eastern Division final in 1969. The Argos won the first game handily, 22–14. Coach Leo Cahill, confident that his team had Ottawa's number, despite the fact that they had only beaten the Riders twice in their last twelve encounters, told the media that "It will take an act of God to beat us on Saturday."

That weekend, the act of God actually occurred. The field at Ottawa's Lansdowne Park was frozen, and the Argos were only equipped with standard cleats and running shoes. The Rough Riders, meanwhile, had broomball style shoes that provided excellent traction on the slippery surface. The Riders pounded the Argos 32–3 to advance to the Grey Cup.

What three Hall of Fame quarterbacks were drafted in 1983?

The 1983 NFL Draft was almost certainly the richest draft ever, in terms of quarterback talent. Three legends of the sport were drafted in the first round: John Elway was selected first overall, Jim Kelly 14th, and Dan Marino 27th. All three went on to Hall of Fame careers.

Three other quarterbacks were selected in the first round that year: Todd Blackledge, Tony Eason, and Ken O'Brien. While Eason took the Patriots to the Super Bowl in 1984 and O'Brien was a two-time Pro Bowl selection, Blackledge's career was unspectacular.

Who was known as "The Intellectual Assassin"?

Ron Mix wasn't a fan of football. He played baseball in high school, and only went on to play football in university because he was given a scholarship by USC. Even when he turned pro, signing with the Los Angeles Chargers of the AFL, he only planned to play for a couple of years.

An offensive tackle with a physical style of play, Mix was dominant, and eventually began to love the game. But he continued his studies and earned a law degree, which he put to use after retiring from the game in 1971.

Incredibly, over his 12-year career, Mix was only called for holding twice.

Who said "Winning isn't everything; it's the only thing"?

While credit is often given to Vince Lombardi, who repeated it many times over the course of his life, it actually originates with Henry Russell "Red" Sanders, the long-time coach of the UCLA Bruins. He first made the comment at a physical education workshop in 1950, saying, "I'll be honest. Winning isn't everything. Men, it's the only thing." Then, in 1955, in an interview with *Sports Illustrated*, he repeated the philosophy, saying, "Sure, winning isn't everything. It's the only thing."

Lombardi's first-known use of the expression didn't come until 1959.

Who was "The Gipper"?

The phrase "Win one for the Gipper" has become a sports cliché. The line was originally uttered by the Gipper himself — George Gipp.

Gipp was a legendary member of the Notre Dame Fighting Irish, playing at multiple positions — most notably, quarterback and halfback. His team-record 2,341 rushing yards stood for more than 50 years.

In late November 1920, Gipp contracted strep throat, which developed into pneumonia. He died on December 14. In his final days, Notre Dame Coach Knute Rockne visited Gipp in the hospital. Gipp reportedly said the following: "Some time, Rock, when the team is up against it, when things are wrong and the breaks are beating the boys, ask them to go in there with all they've got and win just one for the Gipper."

Rockne found the opportunity to fulfill this request prior to a 1928 game against Army, using Gipp's line to inspire the Irish to an upset victory.

Why was George Gipp's body exhumed?

In October 2007, a pair of women asked to have college football legend George "The Gipper" Gipp's body exhumed for DNA testing. They believed that their mother, who had recently passed away, was the daughter of Gipp, conceived out of wedlock with an 18-year-old high school student.

When the results of the testing showed that Gipp and the woman were not related, it touched off a family squabble among relatives of Gipp. A great-nephew had given permission for the exhumation, but two distant cousins claimed he did not have the authority to speak for the entire family, and filed a lawsuit over what they considered a desecration of the grave.

Who was the youngest coach ever to win one hundred games in the NFL?

John Madden achieved his most lasting fame in the broadcast booth, popularizing the word "Doink!" and using his telestrator at every conceivable opportunity. He became so prominent as a colour commentator that *John Madden Football* became the most dominant football product in the gaming market for many years.

Because of his 30 years as a broadcaster, it's almost easy to forget that he was also an outstanding football coach. In 10 years as coach of the Oakland Raiders, between 1969 and 1978, he compiled a 103–32–7 record, winning one Super Bowl. He left coaching at the age of 42 as the youngest coach ever to reach 100 wins.

great
and
not-so-great
moments

What was the "Fog Bowl"?

Toronto's lakeside Exhibition Stadium was always a favourite prey of the elements, and the 1962 Grey Cup was no exception.

The December 1, 1962, game pitted the Hamilton Tiger-Cats against the Winnipeg Blue Bombers. In the second quarter clear skies gave way to a thick fog. Visibility was so poor that not only could fans not see the action, but the players were having trouble. Receivers could not see passes thrown their way, and punt returners had to wait until the ball hit the ground before they could see it.

With the score 28–27 for the Bombers in the fourth quarter, officials gave in and suspended play with just over nine minutes remaining. The game was resumed the following day, December 2, and Winnipeg held on for the win. It was the only game in Grey Cup history to be played over two days.

The name "Fog Bowl" was later borrowed and applied to a 1988 NFL playoff game between the Philadelphia Eagles and the Chicago Bears. While the game was not suspended, visibility was limited to less than 20 yards. The Eagles ultimately prevailed, 20–12.

Whose cereal did Jimmy Johnson stomp on?

When Doug Flutie left the CFL to join the Buffalo Bills in the NFL, a minor mania was touched off, thanks to Flutie's spark plug play on the field. The surge in Flutie's popularity led to the introduction of a new breakfast cereal, Flutie Flakes. Proceeds from sales of the cereal went to the Doug Flutie Jr. Foundation for Autism, which the star quarterback named in honour of his autistic son.

Apparently unaware of the charitable purpose of the cereal, Miami Dolphins coach Jimmy Johnson celebrated

Oops! Famous Fumble #1: Jim Marshall

In a 1964 game against San Francisco, the Minnesota Vikings defensive end recovered a 49ers fumble, and fulfilled a defender's dream: he ran it 66 yards into the end zone. The only problem was that he ran the wrong way, and ended up in his own end zone. Marshall stood dumbfounded in the end zone when his teammates arrived to inform him of his blunder.

his team's victory over Flutie's Bills by pouring a box of Flutie Flakes on the floor of his team's dressing room and stomping on them. Johnson later apologized.

What Monday Night Football commentator was suspected of being intoxicated on-air in the early 1970s?

Embarrassing Gridiron Moment #1

Plaxico Burress is often the centre of attention — sometimes for the wrong reasons. As a rookie with the Steelers in 2000, it was the wrong reasons. In a third down situation in a game against the Jaguars, Burress made a catch to give the Steelers a first down, and fell to the ground. He then got up and spiked the ball. Burress had forgotten that, in the NFL, you're not "down" until an opponent makes contact. The ball was live, the Jaguars recovered.

More than one announcer on the ABC staple was suspected of on-the-job drunkenness in the early years. During a game in 1973, Howard Cosell's speech was noticeably slurred, and he actually left the booth for the entire second half. Officially he was said to have left due to illness, but many believed he was intoxicated.

Don Meredith had two notable incidents of suspected drunkenness. On one occasion in 1973, Monday Night Football was making its first trip to Denver. Meredith said (on-air), "We're in the Mile High City, and so am I." Rumours emerged that he had taken part in some pre-game drinking. Later that season, he was reported to have been drinking for the duration of a game between the Buffalo Bills and the Kansas City Chiefs.

What former NFL player was later accused of taking part in a fight-fixing scheme as a professional boxer?

Mark Gastineau, defensive end for the New York Jets from 1979 to 1988, was one of the top players in the game, making five Pro Bowl appearances and setting a record for most sacks in a season.

He announced his retirement in 1988, citing family reasons.

In the 1990s, Gastineau embarked on a professional boxing career. While his 15–2 record over a five-year period seemed impressive, several of his opponents later claimed that they were paid to take dives.

Who did the Calgary Stampeders ban from a playoff game against the Saskatchewan Roughriders in 2006?

The Calgary Stampeders were surprised by the outrage when they decided to ban Gainer the Gopher, the mascot of the Saskatchewan Roughriders, from entering McMahon Stadium for the 2006 Western Division semi final. Stamps president Ted Hellard said the move was for the good of the Stamps' own mascot, Ralph the Dog.

"Our fans," he said, "have earned the right for us to be led on the field by our own mascot without competition from Gainer."

Gainer had the last laugh, though — albeit from a province away. The Riders overcame a 16-point deficit to defeat the Stampeders, 30–21.

"It's Good!"
Four Famous Field Goals

Adam Vinatieri. Vinatieri kicked a 48-yard field goal on the final play of Super Bowl XXXVI to give the New England Patriots a 20–17 win over the St. Louis Rams.

Tom Dempsey. With two seconds remaining in a critical regular season matchup, Dempsey kicked a record-setting 63-yard crossbar-scraper to give the New Orleans Saints a 19–17 win over the Detroit Lions.

Jim O'Brien. In Super Bowl V, O'Brien kicked a 32-yard field goal with nine seconds remaining as the Baltimore Colts defeated the Dallas Cowboys, 16–13

Lui Passaglia. Passaglia's field goal on the last play of the 1994 Grey Cup won the title for the B.C. Lions as they defeated the Baltimore Stallions, 26–23.

Who is "Mr. Irrelevant"?

While the moniker sounds like an insult, it is, in fact, a good-natured ribbing delivered annually to the last player selected in the NFL Draft.

Paul Salata, a former NCAA and NFL receiver who calls himself a "fan of the underdog," came up with the idea for naming a Mr. Irrelevant in 1976, when he bestowed the honour upon that year's last-selected, Kelvin Kirk, and invited him to come to Salata's home in Newport Beach, California, for Irrelevant Week celebrations. Each year the tradition has continued, and is a popular event on the Newport Beach calendar.

Each year's Mr. Irrelevant is awarded the Lowsman Trophy, which is a near-replica of the Heisman Trophy — the difference being that the Lowsman figure is fumbling the football.

Who coached both teams during
a college football game?

In 1893, college football was decidedly less formal and organized than it is now. T.L. Bayne was head coach for Tulane and assistant coach for Louisiana State that year, travelling back and forth between campuses. For an encounter on November 25, the regular head coach for LSU, Charles E. Coates, was unavailable, and Bayne did double-duty as coach of both teams. Legend has it that he was also responsible for ticket sales and building the goalposts for the game, and that his payment was a green umbrella.

> **Embarrassing Gridiron Moment #2**
> Bill Gramatica of the Arizona Cardinals got pretty excited about his field goal against the Giants in a 2001 game, though nobody was quite sure why. The score came in the first quarter to give the Cardinals a 3–0 lead. Hardly a significant event. Nevertheless, Gramatica was elated, and leapt in the air to celebrate. When he landed, he tore a ligament in his knee and was out for the season.

Who first called the winning play of the 1972 AFC
Championship Game "the Immaculate Reception"?

Trailing 7–6 to the Oakland Raiders with 22 seconds to play in the fourth quarter, the Pittsburgh Steelers faced a fourth and ten situation on their own 40-yard line. Quarterback Terry Bradshaw, unable to find his primary receiver, opted to throw the ball to fullback John Fuqua. Fuqua was hit as the ball arrived, and the pass was deflected into the arms of running back Franco Harris, who carried the ball all the way into the Raiders end zone for a game winning touchdown.

The play was controversial. Many felt the ball actually hit the intended receiver, Fuqua. Under an NFL rule in place at the time, the play would have been illegal as the same pass had been touched by two receivers in succession. However, the officials ruled that the ball had bounced off the Raiders defender, and the touchdown stood.

Afterwards, a pair of Steelers season-ticket holders, Sharon Levosky and Michael Ord, called the team's radio announcer on his postgame show and suggested the miraculous play be known as the "Immaculate Reception."

Who scored all the points — for both teams — in a college game in 1935?

On December 7, 1935, the University of Washington took on USC, in what turned out to be a low-scoring affair. Byron Haines, a Washington halfback, scored the game's only touchdown, while the USC offence was held scoreless. However, the USC defence did manage to push Haines into the end zone for a safety — their only points — as Haines defeated Haines, 6–2.

"Wide Right!"
Four Famous Missed Field Goals

Scott Norwood. In the dying moments of Super Bowl XXV, the Buffalo Bills quarterback missed a 47-yard attempt, and the Bills lost 20–19.

Gary Anderson. In the NFC Championship Game on January 17, 1999, Anderson missed a 38-yard attempt late in the game that would have cinched a win for the Minnesota Vikings. Instead, the Atlanta Falcons followed the miss with a 71-yard drive that culminated in a game-tying touchdown. The Falcons won in overtime.

Mike Vanderjagt. The Indianapolis Colts kicker missed a 46-yard attempt with 18 seconds left in an AFC Divisional Playoff game against the Pittsburgh Steelers on January 14, 2006. The Colts lost the game, 21–18.

Paul McCallum. The Saskatchewan Roughriders kicker missed an 18-yard attempt in overtime of a playoff game against the B.C. Lions. The Lions went on to win the game.

What game was moved to the day after U.S. Thanksgiving in 1984 to please network television?

As the 1984 U.S. college football season began to unfold, the University of Miami and Boston College were set for a showdown on September 29. Both teams featured marquis quarterbacks: Miami had Bernie Kosar, and Boston College had Doug Flutie.

CBS, the network scheduled to broadcast the game, was salivating, anticipating solid ratings. But they were even more intrigued about the idea of maximizing those ratings by moving the game to November 23, the Friday after U.S. Thanksgiving. That day, Miami was scheduled to play Rutgers.

CBS convinced the schools to adjust their schedules, paying Rutgers a reported $80,000. The result? One of the most famous games in college football history — the "Hail Flutie" game.

Who caught Doug Flutie's Hail Mary pass when Boston College defeated Miami in 1984?

After the University Miami scored a touchdown with 28 seconds remaining to take a 45–41 lead, it looked like they had secured a victory over Boston College. When Boston College's final drive seemed stalled at the Miami 48-yard line with six seconds to play, the BC fate seemed sealed.

Then, on the final play of the game, quarterback Doug Flutie took the snap, dropped back, eluded a tackler, and from his own 36-yard line found Gerry Phelan in the end zone to win the game.

> **Embarrassing Gridiron Moment #3**
>
> Phil Luckett, NFL official, inadvertently made fast friends with the Detroit Lions during a Thanksgiving game against Pittsburgh. During the coin toss that preceded overtime, the Steelers' Jerome Bettis called "tails." However, Luckett thought he'd heard "heads," and the erroneously awarded the toss to Detroit. The Lions chose to receive, and scored a game-winning field goal on their first possession.

What was the Great Rose Bowl Hoax?

Students at the California Institute of Technology (Caltech) often joked that their football team played in front of more empty seats than any team in the nation. After all, they played at the massive Rose Bowl, but garnered little attention or fan interest.

A group of Caltech students — later named the "Fiendish Fourteen" — grew tired of being ignored while the stadium and its annual game achieved nationwide fame. Prior to the 1961 Rose Bowl Game, they learned that cheerleaders for one of the competing teams, the Washington Huskies, had planned a special gimmick for halftime. Spectators were given cards that they were to hold over their heads — each card being coloured as part of an overall

> **Oops! Famous Fumble #2: Leon Lett**
>
> In Super Bowl XXVII, Lett of the Dallas Cowboys recovered a fumble and ran the ball towards the end zone. Thinking he was in the clear, he decided to showboat and attempted to run parallel to the goal line and hold the ball out for a touchdown. He was caught by Buffalo's Don Beebe and fumbled. Lott later said that he was watching himself on the Jumbotron and was trying to imitate a hotdog move he'd seen teammate Michael Irvin perform.

Oops! Famous Fumble #3: Earnest Byner

Late in the AFC Championship Game in 1988, the Cleveland Browns' Byner took a handoff with 1:12 remaining and was headed for the end zone when he allowed Denver defensive back Jeremiah Castille to strip him of the ball on the three-yard line. The Broncos won the game, and Byner the scorn of Browns fans.

pattern that would display images for the delight of television viewers.

The night before the game the Fiendish Fourteen broke into the cheerleaders' hotel rooms and replaced the cards with ones of their own.

At halftime, when the cards were raised, some of the cheerleaders' planned images remained intact, but the Huskies logo was replaced by a Caltech Beavers logo, and the word "Caltech" was raised at one end of the stadium. The cheerleaders were not amused.

Who scarred the left eye of a future American president?

U.S. president Gerald Ford was often mocked by comedians for his apparent clumsiness, but at least one of his injuries was sustained in an intentional act of athleticism.

Embarrassing Gridiron Moment #4

The Fifth Down. A 1990 Big 12 Conference matchup pitted the Colorado Buffaloes against the Missouri Tigers. On first and goal, Colorado ran two plays that failed to find the end zone. Though it SHOULD have been third down, the sideline markers indicated second down. After a fail to run into the end zone, time was winding down, and Colorado quarterback Charles Johnson spiked the ball to stop the clock. That should have been the fourth down. The officials trusted the sideline markers, and on the next play — the fifth down — Colorado scored a touchdown. The score won the game, and helped Colorado earn a share of the National Championship.

Ford was a centre for the University of Michigan. In 1934, Michigan played the University of Chicago, who featured the first-ever Heisman Trophy winner, Jay Berwanger. Ford tackled Berwanger, but Berwanger's heel caught Ford's cheekbone, opening a three-inch gash. The incident left a scar that Ford carried with him the rest of his life.

Who was the recipient of the first "Gatorade shower"?

During their 1986 season and run toward a Super Bowl title, the New York

Giants became known for celebrating big wins by dumping an icy bucket of Gatorade on head coach Bill Parcells. The ritual received massive attention in the media and became a phenomenon that spread throughout the sport at every level — thanks to the ingenuity of Parcells and the Giants.

Or not. The story of the tradition beginning with the 1986 Giants is a myth. The first Gatorade shower actually took place two years earlier when the 1984 Chicago Bears were on the verge of clinching the Central Division title. Steve McMichael grabbed coach Mike Ditka, while Mike Singeltary and Dan Hampton moved in and dumped the Gatorade bucket on him. For years, the Bears were content to let the Giants take the credit, until 1999, when Hampton, fed up with the misattributed recognition, told the story to the *Daily Herald* in Chicago. The *Daily Herald* went to the game tapes and confirmed Hampton's claim.

Who were the passer and receiver on the 1982 play known as "The Catch"?

The San Francisco 49ers trailed the Dallas Cowboys 27–21 with less than a minute to play in the 1982 NFC Championship Game. On third down from the Cowboys' six-yard line, Joe Montana took the snap and looked for his intended receiver, Freddie Solomon. But Solomon was covered, and Montana had to scramble to escape rushing Cowboys defenders. He spotted the secondary receiver, Dwight Clark, and lofted a pass to the right side of the end zone that appeared to be out of reach. But Clark leapt, grasped the ball with his fingertips, and pulled it down for the game-winning touchdown.

Oops! Famous Fumble #4: Joe Pisarcik

In a late-season game against the Philadelphia Eagles, all Pisarcik needed to do was take a knee and allow time to expire, and the New York Giants would have a victory. The network covering the game was already running the credits. But a strange sideline call intended to protect the quarterback from being hit called for a handoff to Larry Czonka. The incredulous Czonka told Pisarcik it was a senseless risk, and vowed that he wouldn't accept the handoff if Pisarcik went through with it. Fearing the wrath of the offensive coordinator, Pisarcik tried to hand off to Czonka, but it bounced off the fullback's hip and went to the ground. The Eagles recovered and returned the fumble for a game-winning touchdown.

The play soon became known as "The Catch," and is one of the most storied plays in NFL history.

Who was the ball carrier on the final play of Super Bowl XXXIV in 2000?

After falling behind the St. Louis Rams 23–16 late in the game, quarterback Steve McNair led his Tennessee Titans down to the Rams' 10-yard line with only six seconds remaining. With no timeouts, the Titans had one play to find the end zone and force overtime.

McNair passed to an open Kevin Dyson at the five-yard line, but Mike Jones, covering another player, spotted the pass and turned to grab Dyson's legs. Dyson reached in vain for the goal line, but was brought down at the one-yard line as time expired.

Quickies
Did you know ...

The Super Bowl XXXVI was the first Super Bowl played in February? Prior to that, all Super Bowls had been played in January. Since that time, all but one (Super Bowl XXXVII) has been played in February.

What was the "Ice Bowl"?

The Green Bay Packers' home stadium, Lambeau Field, is often referred to as "The Frozen Tundra." Never was this nickname more apt than in the 1967 NFL Championship Game between the host Packers and the Dallas Cowboys.

With a game-time temperature of -13ºF (-25ºC), it was the coldest game ever played in the NFL, without wind chill being taken into account. It was so cold that the turf heating system failed, and the field was rock-hard. The officials were unable to use their whistles as they froze to their lips, and so, they had to replace whistle-blowing with shouting.

The game itself was a classic. The Cowboys overcame a 14–0 deficit to take a 17–14 lead in the fourth quarter. Then, with six seconds remaining on the clock, Packers quarterback Bart Starr executed a quarterback sneak and ran into the end zone for a 21–17 win, and the Packers' third straight NFL Championship.

What was memorable about the 1948 Grey Cup?

The fact that the Calgary Stampeders won the 1948 Grey Cup in Toronto and completed a perfect season is almost a side note. The game itself featured memorable moments, such as the "sitting touchdown," a trick play in which receiver Norm Hill lay on his back in the end zone, virtually hidden, then sat up to receive the touchdown pass. But the real excitement occurred at the Royal York Hotel, where celebrating Stampeders fans carried the goal posts into the lobby and rode horses through the front doors and onto the elevators.

Embarrassing Gridiron Moment #5
Phil Luckett. Poor Phil has the honour of being in our Embarrassing Gridiron Moments list twice. This time, the official was working a New Orleans-Carolina game in 2001. Joe Horn, receiver for the Saints, was delighted to be in the open in the end zone with a pass coming his way. Little did he know that he WAS covered ... by Luckett. The ball hit Luckett in the head, and fell incomplete.

Who fumbled in the dying minutes of the 1971 Grey Cup?

The hard-luck Toronto Argonauts had not won a Grey Cup since 1952, but were on the verge of ending their drought in 1971. Led by future NFL great Joe Theismann, the Argos advanced to the Grey Cup against the Calgary Stampeders. Late in the game, trailing 14–11, the Argos' Dick Thornton intercepted a Stamps past and returned it to their 11-yard line. After advancing a further four yards, the Argos elected to run on second down to ensure a chance to tie the game with a field goal if they were unable to find the end zone.

Theismann handed off to Leon McQuay, who saw an opening and headed for the end zone. Just then, his foot slipped on the wet turf and his elbow hit the ground, jarring the ball

Embarrassing Gridiron Moment #6
Gus Frerotte. Purists complain about players doing dances to celebrate touchdowns, but most would probably have preferred to see Gus Frerotte dance instead of his celebration of choice. As a member of the Washington Redskins in 1997, Frerotte ran for a touchdown and decided that a really cool way to celebrate would be to slam his head into the padded wall behind the end zone. The resulting neck injury ended his season.

loose. The Stampeders recovered and won the game, while the Argos would have to wait another 12 years to break their Grey Cup drought.

What was the "Freezer Bowl"?

The name "Ice Bowl" had already been taken, but with the wind chill temperatures being what they were, those present thought that giving the 1981 AFC Championship a name of its own was only appropriate.

The game pitted the San Diego Chargers against the Cincinnati Bengals. The Bengals were favoured largely because they had a better record, and had blown out the Chargers in the regular season. But the fact that the Bengals played in a cold-weather climate while the Chargers were more accustomed to the milder temperatures of California would only work in Cincinnati's favour.

Game time temperature was -9°F (-23°C), but it was the wind chill that made conditions particularly brutal. With sustained winds of 27 miles per hour, the wind chill was calculated as -59°F (-51°C), making it the coldest game in terms of wind chill in NFL history.

The favoured Bengals won the game, 27–7.

firsts and record-breakers

Who were the first inductees into the Pro Football Hall of Fame?

When the Pro Football Hall of Fame first opened its doors on September 7, 1963, a whopping 17 members were enshrined as the first inductees. They were: Sammy Baugh, Bert Bell, Joe Carr, Earl "Dutch" Clark, Harold "Red" Grange, George Halas, Mel Hein, Wilbur "Pete" Henry, Robert "Cal" Hubbard, Don Hutson, Earl "Curly" Lambeau, Tim Mara, George Preston Marshall, John "Blood" McNally, Bronko Nagurski, Ernie Nevers, and Jim Thorpe.

From the Record Books:
Career Rushing Yards Leaders

NFL

Emmitt Smith	18,355
Walter Payton	16,726
Barry Sanders	15,269

CFL

Mike Pringle	16,425
George Reed	16,116
Damon Allen	11,920

Who was professional football's first superstar?

Jim Thorpe was already a household name long before playing professional football. The versatile, multi-sport athlete had received a tickertape parade down Broadway in New York after winning gold medals in the pentathlon and decathlon at the 1912 Olympic Games. The following year, he was stripped of his medals after it was learned that he had played two seasons of professional baseball in the East Carolina League.

In 1913, Thorpe signed with the New York Giants baseball team, playing with them for three seasons. In 1915, he became a member of professional football's Canton Bulldogs. With Thorpe's arrival, the team's attendance skyrocketed from an average of 1,200 fans a game to 8,000. Thorpe helped lead the team to three titles before Canton became one of the founding members of the American Professional Football Association — soon renamed the National Football League — in 1920. Thorpe continued playing on several NFL teams until retiring in 1928. In 1950, the Associated Press named him the top American athlete of the first half of the twentieth century.

What was the lowest-scoring team in NFL history?

The 1942 Detroit Lions were a terrible team, going 0–11 and scoring only 38 points all season. This putrid performance was matched only by the 1933 Cincinnati Reds, who accomplished the feat in 10 games, but, remarkably, were able to win three times and tie once.

The following season, the Reds were an even worse team, and scored only 10 points in eight games before having their franchise revoked and replaced with the St. Louis Gunners for the remainder of the season. Officially, the Reds-Gunners records were counted as one, and the teams combined for 37 points in 11 games.

But the all-time champions of offensive ineptitude were the 1928 Chicago Cardinals, who managed a 7–0 win over the hapless Dayton Triangles in the second game of the season, but didn't score a single point in any of their five other games, finishing with a 1–5 record, and a mere seven points in six games.

What was the first non-Canadian team to win the Grey Cup?

> **Quickies**
> *Did you know ...*
> That the Pittsburgh Steelers have hosted more conference championship games (10) than any other team? The San Francisco 49ers have hosted the most NFC Championship Games (eight).

A shining light amid an otherwise dismal attempt by the CFL to expand south of the border, the Baltimore football club (playing without a name) made a splash in their first season, reaching the 1994 Grey Cup against the B.C. Lions. However, they lost on a field goal by Vancouver-born Lui Passaglia on the last play of the game.

The following year, now playing as the Baltimore Stallions, they reached the Grey Cup again, prevailing over the Calgary Stampeders, 37–20.

Who holds the record for the longest field goal?

At the professional level, two men are tied for the longest-ever field goal at 63 yards. Tom Dempsey first accomplished this feat on November 8,

1970. Kicking with a club foot that had no toes, he nailed the 63-yard attempt with two seconds left on the clock as the New Orleans Saints defeated the Detroit Lions 19–17. It was one of only two wins for the Saints that year. Dempsey's record was matched on October 25, 1998, by Jason Elam of the Denver Broncos.

The longest field goal in history, at any level, was kicked by Ove Johansson of Abilene Christian University in the NAIA on October 16, 1976. It turned out to be the peak of Johansson's football career. While he did manage to catch on with the NFL's Philadelphia Eagles, his stint was short-lived and disastrous. He appeared in only two games, and was one for four in field goal attempts, and one for three in extra-point attempts.

From the Record Books:
Career Passing Yards Leaders

NFL	
Brett Favre	61,655
Dan Marino	61,361
John Elway	51,475

CFL	
Damon Allen	72,381
Danny McManus	53,165
Anthony Calvillo	53,050

Who was the first player to receive the Rose Bowl Player of the Game Award?

In the official list of Rose Bowl Players of the Game, Neil Snow is listed as the outstanding performer in the first Rose Bowl in 1902. However, the award was not actually established until 1953, and was "awarded" to past stars retroactively. Snow, who died in 1914, never knew he had received the honour.

The first player to actually receive the Player of the Game award was USC quarterback Rudy Bukich, who stepped into the game after the Trojans' starting quarterback was injured and led his team to a 7–0 win.

What was the largest single-game attendance in NFL history?

The NFL has experimented with international games on several occasions, but the October 2, 2005, regular season game between the

San Francisco 49ers and the Arizona Cardinals, in Mexico City, was the greatest success, at least in terms of attendance.

An NFL-record 103,467 fans filled Azteca Stadium to see the Cardinals knock off the 49ers, 31–14.

Despite the huge crowd, the NFL has no immediate plans to expand into Mexico. Commissioner Paul Tagliabue, commenting on the possibility of a team in Mexico City, said, "I think it will happen, probably in our lifetime, but I'm hoping to live a long time."

> **Quickies**
> **Did you know ...**
> That the Superdome in New Orleans has hosted the most Super Bowls (six)? But Miami is the city that has played host most often (nine times), albeit in more than one venue.

Who has won the most Super Bowls?

Thanks to two championships in the 2000s, the Pittsburgh Steelers hold the record for the most Super Bowl wins with six. Their nearest challengers are the Dallas Cowboys and San Francisco 49ers, both of whom have won five Super Bowls.

As far as individual players go, Charles Haley has won the most Super Bowl rings, winning twice as a San Francisco 49er and three times as a Dallas Cowboy.

Who has won the most Grey Cups?

If we count the entire history of the Grey Cup, including the years prior to the CFL when amateur teams competed for the trophy, the Toronto Argonauts lead the pack with fifteen Grey Cup wins.

It is generally felt, though, that the modern era of Canadian football didn't begin until the mid-fifties, by which time the championship was played exclusively between professional teams in the organizations that, a few years later, became known as the Canadian Football League.

Beginning in 1954, the Edmonton Eskimos have been the winningest team in Grey Cup history, taking the trophy home 12 times.

When was the first Grey Cup played?

On December 4, 1909, the University of Toronto met the Parkdale Canoe Club at Rosedale field to determine the Rugby Football Championship of Canada. Although Lord Earl Grey's trophy was not ready yet, it had already been determined that the winner of this game would be the inaugural recipient of the Grey Cup. Led by kicker Hugh Gall, who kicked a record eight singles, the University of Toronto team prevailed by a score of 26–6 before a crowd of 3,807.

When was the first Vanier Cup played?

When originally conceived, the Vanier Cup was the name of the trophy awarded to the winner of the Canadian College Bowl. The idea was similar to American college bowl games: two teams would be invited by a panel to play for what was being called the "national championship," despite the absence of a playoff system.

The first winners of the Vanier Cup were the University of Toronto, who defeated the University of Alberta 14–7 at Toronto's Varsity Stadium.

After two years, the game came under the direction of the Canadian Interuniversity Athletic Union (CIAU — now known as Canadian Interuniversity Sports). A playoff system was developed, and the invitation format was abandoned. The first winners under the new playoff system were the University of Alberta, who triumphed 10–9 over McMaster University.

Who has won the most Vanier Cups?

The University of Western Ontario Mustangs have won the most Vanier Cup Championships, taking home the hardware six times. They have stiff competition from the University of Laval Rouge et Or, however. As of 2008, Laval had won the trophy five times, and were one of the powerhouses of Canadian football.

The nearest challengers after Laval are the University of Calgary, with four Vanier wins, and several teams who are tied with three wins.

Who has won the most American college National Championships?

From the Record Books:
Most Career Yards Gained

NFL
Jerry Rice	22,895
Tim Brown	14,934
Isaac Bruce	14,109

CFL
Allen Pitts	14,891
Milt Stegall	14,695
Darren Flutie	14,359

The waters of National Championship are muddied by the numerous polls that have existed over the years, which have included consensus and non-consensus champions, championships awarded retroactively, championships awarded prior to the playing of bowl games, and even polls that have changed their minds.

If we tally up all the national championships awarded by various major selectors dating back to 1869, Princeton has the most National Championships with 28, followed by Yale with 27.

Ivy League schools are not the football powerhouses they once were, however, and many prefer to measure the number of championships won by schools currently part of the Football Bowl System of NCAA Division I. Going that route, Notre Dame leads the pack with 12 National Championships, followed by Alabama with 11.

Quickies
Did you know ...

That more pizza is sold on Super Bowl Sunday than on any other day of the year? It sounds like a tough gig for the poor pizza-delivery person who has to miss the game, but there is a bright side: tips also skyrocket on Super Sunday.

What was the first NFL team to have cheerleaders and a mascot?

The Baltimore Colts of the late 1950s produced a number of NFL firsts, including the first fan clubs (the Colt Corrals) and the first helmet logos. They were also the first NFL team to have cheerleaders and a mascot. The mascot was, originally, a live horse named Dixie who would do a victory lap around the stadium after every Baltimore touchdown. Dixie was later replaced by two humans in a horse suit.

What was the first football team to play on artificial turf?

When the Houston Astrodome first opened in 1965 the field was made from natural grass. However, baseball outfielders found that the glass panels in the dome's ceiling — which were necessary in order to keep the grass alive — created a glare that made fielding impossible, and the panels were painted over. This meant it was necessary to install artificial grass in the stadium.

The first football game played on artificial turf saw the University of Houston take on Washington State on September 23, 1966.

Who was the first African-American to play in the NFL?

In the early days of the NFL, there was no official colour barrier, though African-American players were not commonplace. When the NFL (known then as the American Professional Football Association) began play in 1920, two African-Americans took the field: the Akron Pros' Frederick "Fritz" Pollard and the Rock Island Independents' Bobby Marshall.

But in the 1930s, things changed. George Preston Marshall, owner of the Boston Braves (who later became the Washington Redskins) refused to allow African-Americans on his team, and put pressure on other owners to adopt the same policy. By 1934, no African-American players were on the rosters of any team in the NFL.

In 1946 the colour barrier was broken when the Cleveland Rams moved to Los Angeles. The team was to play in the Los Angeles Coliseum, but the commissioners of the stadium had a major stipulation: the team had to be racially integrated. Woody Strode and Kenny Washington — UCLA alumni who played college football with baseball's Jackie Robinson — debuted that season as the first African-American players in the NFL's modern era.

What Canadian has scored the most points in the CFL?

Vancouver-born Lui Passaglia is not only the all-time leader among Canadians, but has scored more points than any player in any professional sports league. In 408 career games as placekicker and punter — all with the BC Lions — Passaglia amassed 3,991 points.

Passaglia's most famous moment came in the 1994 Grey Cup when he kicked a Cup-winning field goal on the last play of the game.

From the Record Books: Most Career Touchdowns

NFL	
Jerry Rice	208
Emmitt Smith	175
Marcus Allen	145

CFL	
Milt Stegall	144
George Reed	137
Mike Pringle	137

What college has produced the most NFL players?

Footballers looking for the best path to the pros will want to take note. As of the beginning of the 2009 season, the University of Notre Dame has had the most alumni appear in the NFL, with 459. Next in line is the University of Southern California with 441.

When was the first NFL regular-season game played outside the United States?

In recent years, the Buffalo Bills gained the ire of some fans by choosing to play one game each year in Toronto. But the Bills' international experiment was not the first time that the NFL has staged regular-season games outside the United States.

The first such international venture took place in 2005 when the Arizona Cardinals took on the San Francisco 49ers before a crowd of 103,467 in Mexico City. The Cardinals won, 31–14.

When was the first CFL game played outside Canada?

The collapse of the original World League of American Football was followed shortly by the CFL's first attempt at expansion into the United States. Fred Anderson, owner of the WLAF's Sacramento Surge, jumped at the chance to be among the first American teams in the Canadian league. He started a new team, the Sacramento Gold Miners, using similar uniforms and some of the same players as his old WLAF team.

Originally the CFL planned to have multiple American teams in the 1993 season, but only the Gold Miners were ready to take the field.

The Gold Miners played a short pre-season schedule and two road games before playing host to the first CFL game outside of Canada on July 17, 1993. They lost to the Calgary Stampeders, 38–36.

Two years later, the Gold Miners moved to San Antonio, where they lasted one year before folding.

How many coaches have won the Super Bowl and U.S. college football's National Championship?

In the 1992 season, the Dallas Cowboys won their first of two consecutive Super Bowls. Their head coach was Jimmy Johnson, who, having already won a National Championship with the 1987 University of Miami Hurricanes, became the first person to coach teams to college National Championships and Super Bowl wins.

After the Boys' second Super Bowl win, Johnson and Cowboys owner Jerry Jones agreed to part ways, as their working relationship had become unmanageable. Johnson was replaced by Barry Switzer, who had won college National Championships as coach of the Oklahoma Sooners.

In the 1995 season, Switzer coached the Cowboys to a 12–4 record, and the team went on to win the Super Bowl.

Johnson and Switzer remain the only coaches to have won National Championships and the Super Bowl.

What was the biggest comeback in NFL history?

On January 3, 1993, the Buffalo Bills hosted the Houston Oilers in the Wildcard game. The Bills were hoping to use the game as a stepping stone to their third consecutive Super Bowl appearance, but with star quarterback Jim Kelly out with a ligament injury, Frank Reich was called into action.

It looked like a disaster. The Oilers, with Warren Moon as quarterback, surged to an early lead, and by the third quarter held a devastating 35–3 lead.

But this was familiar territory for Frank Reich. In 1984, while still a college player, he had lead the Maryland Terrapins to a stunning comeback against the Miami Hurricanes, turning a 31–0 deficit into a 42–40 win.

Drawing on the spirits of comebacks past, the Bills scored 28 points in the third quarter. In the fourth quarter, an Andre Reed touchdown gave the Bills the lead, though it was countered by an Oiler field goal, sending the game into overtime. Steve Christie then kicked a 32-yard field goal to complete the biggest comeback in NFL history, turning a 32-point deficit into a 41–38 win.

Who won the first Heisman Trophy, and why did he never play professionally?

Jay Berwanger was a multisport athlete at the University of Chicago. A track and field star, he set a school decathlon record that stood for more than 70 years. But his lasting fame in the sporting world came from two firsts as a football player: in 1935 he was the first recipient of the Heisman Trophy (then called the Downtown Athletic Club Trophy); a year later he became the first player ever drafted into the National Football League.

But after being drafted by the Philadelphia Eagles, the Chicago Bears acquired his rights. Berwanger asked the Bears for $25,000 over two years, and Coach George Halas felt that such a salary was too high. Berwanger opted to forego a football career, instead becoming a foam-rubber salesman.

What was the first college bowl game?

The first college bowl game was not actually referred to as a "bowl" game, and did not even go by its present name until more than two decades after the annual game was first played.

On January 1, 1902, the tradition of New Year's Day college football clashes began when Michigan overwhelmed Stanford 49–0 in what was called the Tournament East-West Football Game. The beating was so severe that Stanford actually quit after three quarters, and the "annual" game was scrubbed for the next 14 years.

In 1916, the game was revived and the State College of Washington defeated Brown College. From then on, the game was held every year, but it did undergo a major change. After the original host facility for the game — Tournament Park — was deemed unsuitable, the game moved to a new stadium, and that stadium gave the annual game its new name: the Rose Bowl.

What team has won the most Rose Bowls?

From the Record Books:
Most Career Combined Yards Goals

NFL

Jerry Rice	23,546
Brian Mitchell	23,330
Walter Payton	21,803

CFL

Mike "Pinball" Clemons	25,438
Henry "Gizmo" Williams	23,927
Mike Pringle	23,208

Given that they have also appeared in far more games than any other school, it comes as no surprise that the University of Southern California also has the most Rose Bowl wins, taking home the title 24 times in 33 appearances, as of 2009. The nearest competitor is the University of Michigan with eight wins in 20 games.

Who was the first Wildcard team to win the Super Bowl?

The Wildcard format in American professional football was first introduced in the AFL in 1969, prior to the completion of the NFL-AFL merger. That year, the Kansas City Chiefs won the Wildcard and took advantage by beating the AFL East champion New York Jets 13–6. They followed this effort with a victory over the Oakland Raiders to win the final AFL championship.

The Chiefs capped their post-season run in the fourth AFL-NFL Championship Game (since renamed SuperBowl IV). The Chiefs laid a 23–7 drubbing on the favoured Minnesota Vikings.

What team has the most number of inductees in the Pro Football Hall of Fame?

With representation from such legends as George Halas, Red Grange, Dick Butkus, and Walter Payton, the Chicago Bears have had the most players and executives elected to the Pro Football Hall of Fame, with 26. Their nearest competitors are the Green Bay Packers, who boast 21 hall of famers.

Who is the winningest coach in CFL history?

Don Matthews, who coached six different teams in the CFL, amassed the most wins of any coach with 231.

In addition to his overall win totals, Matthews also holds the record for most Grey Cup appearances (nine) and most Grey Cup wins (five).

Who is the winningest coach in NFL history?

Don Shula, the long-time coach of the Miami Dolphins, racked up an astonishing total of 328 victories over the course of his career, including the only perfect season in NFL history in 1972.

But for all his victories, he does not hold the record for most Super Bowl wins. That honour goes to Chuck Knoll, the man at the helm of the Pittsburgh Steelers dynasty that won four Super Bowls in six years between 1975 and 1980.

Who is the winningest coach in NCAA history?

Longevity has its merits, and Joe Paterno, who, as of the end of the 2008 season, had coached the Penn State Nittany Lions for 59 years, has the records to prove it. Between 1966 and 2008, Penn State teams won 383 games under Paterno's stewardship. He also holds the record for most Bowl victories with 23. Along the way, he has won two National Championships and three Big Ten Championships.

Paterno had opportunities to take his coaching skills to professional football — he was offered head coaching positions with the Pittsburgh Steelers and the New England Patriots (the latter included an offer of part-ownership), but he elected to remain with Penn State, and is currently signed to coach the team through the 2011 season. He will be 85 years old upon the completion of his contract.

Who is the winningest coach in Arena Football League history?

While the Arena Football League does not get as much attention as other professional leagues, the accomplishments of some of their members are impressive. One of the most impressive Arena Leaguers is coach Tim Marcum. As head coach of the Denver Dynamite in 1987, the Detroit Drive from 1988 to 1993, and the Tampa Bay Storm from 1994 on,

From the Record Books:
Most Career Sacks

NFL
Bruce Smith	200.0
Reggie White	198.0
Kevin Greene	160.0

CFL
Grover Covington	157.0
Elfrid Payton	154.0
Bobby Jurasin	142.0

he has won more than 160 games. Even more impressive, he has guided teams into the ArenaBowl final 10 times, winning seven times. That's all the more remarkable when you consider that, as of 2008, only 21 ArenaBowls have been played in total.

Marcum was inducted into the AFL Hall of Fame in 1998.

leagues of the past

What was the USFL?

The United States Football league was founded by New Orleans businessman and sports executive Dave Dixon, who was instrumental in the formation of the New Orleans Saints. The USFL was an attempt to provide a spring alternative to the NFL. The formation of the league was announced at the 21 Club in New York City on May 11, 1982. Play began the following year.

Originally, the league was made up of 12 teams, all located in large markets: Los Angeles, San Diego, Oakland, New York, New Jersey, Chicago, Detroit, Boston, Birmingham, Denver, Philadelphia, and Tampa Bay. The league had contracts with ABC and ESPN, and the ratings were good. Attendance was low in the first season, but was on the rise by year two.

Unfortunately, the only two teams to make money were the Tampa Bay Bandits and the Denver Gold (who had the highest league attendance). The rest of the teams lost money, mostly due to larger than anticipated player salaries. During the second season the league expanded, but the money troubles continued.

In 1986, before making a planned switch to a fall schedule, the NSFL finally folded. By then more than $160 million in debt had been accrued.

Why did the USFL sue the NFL?

The USFL was on shaky ground after just three seasons, and they made a decision to become a fall league in 1986, in direct competition with the NFL. But it was not to be. The USFL could not get networks to cover their games, and many teams were in deep financial trouble.

The USFL blamed the NFL for its woes, and launched an antitrust suit, claiming that the NFL engaged in predatory practices. Among other things, the NFL was accused of using its influence to limit the USFL's access to venues and network broadcast deals, and targeting the league as a whole and franchises in particular in an attempt to squash the competing league.

A jury found in favour of the USFL, but awarded the fledgling league only $1 in compensation. The league put its 1986 season on hold, and ultimately folded.

What was the XFL?

The XFL was the much-mocked attempt by World Wrestling Federation owner Vince McMahon to establish an American football league to rival the NFL.

Like the earlier USFL, the XFL set itself up as a spring league to avoid direct competition with the NFL. But it was clear from the start that the gloves were off, as the XFL encouraged its players to be an over-the-top alternative to the "No Fun League." Touchdown celebrations were encouraged, roughing penalties were limited, and stadium announcers were encouraged to taunt the opposition. Pre-game coin tosses were replaced by players fighting for a ball, and that sissy fair catch rule was eliminated.

Curiosity drew 14 million viewers to the league's debut game between the New York/New Jersey Hitmen and the Las Vegas Outlaws on February 3, 2001. But few fans were impressed by the new product, and ratings and attendance dwindled as the season went on.

After only one season, the league folded.

What was Paul McCallum's jersey name in the XFL?

Vancouver-born kicker Paul McCallum spent most of his career in the CFL, but spent one year with the WLAF's Scottish Claymores in 1996, and was a member of the XFL's Las Vegas Outlaws in 2001. Playing in the "fun" league that allowed players to put whatever they wanted in place of their name on their jersey, McCallum chose the nickname "CFL Reject."

McCallum was actually anything but a reject as a CFLer, and he returned to Canada following the demise of the XFL. It was not a flawless return, however. In 2004, as a member of the Saskatchewan Roughriders, he became infamous for missing an 18-yard field goal in overtime. The Riders lost the game, and irate fans vandalized the kicker's home. He was subsequently mocked (to his face) on the Canadian comedy program *This Hour Has 22 Minutes* when a cast member called McCallum "a bum who could be outkicked by a goat missing a leg." McCallum had the last laugh, though. In 2006 he set a CFL record by kicking a 62-yard field goal. Later that year, he tied the record for the most field goals in a Grey Cup, making six kicks in six attempts, winning the MVP award.

Who won the Most Valuable Player Award in the XFL's first and only championship game?

Jose Cortez, the placekicker for the Los Angeles Xtreme, kicked three field goals to help his team to a 38–6 drubbing of the San Francisco Demons, in the first and only XFL Championship Game in 2001. He was also the league's leading scorer that season, having kicked 20 field goals.

Ironically, despite his value to his team, kickers under the XFL's pay structure were the lowest-paid players in the league.

The much-travelled kicker also spent time in the NFL, the Arena Football League, and NFL Europe.

What was He Hate Me's real name?

The XFL was a league of gimmicks, few of which caught the public's attention. But one player took advantage of one of the gimmicks and rode it to his 15 minutes of fame.

The XFL encouraged players to use nicknames and phrases on their jerseys, instead of their real names. The grammatically challenged Rod Smart, making his professional football debut, chose the words "He Hate Me" for the

XFL Players Who Also Played in the NFL

John Avery
Ron Carpenter
Jose Cortez
Eric England
Mike Furrey
Steve Gleason
Kelly Herndon
Corey Ivy
Kevin Kaesviharn
Tommy Maddox
Yo Murphy
Rashaan Salaam
Kevin Swayne
Rod Smart
Brad Trout

XFL Players Who Also Played in the CFL

Kelvin Anderson
John Avery
Duane Butler
Jermaine Copeland
Marcus Crandell
Reggie Durden
Eric England
Paul McCallum
Yo Murphy
Noel Prefontaine
Bobby Singh

back of his jersey. His explanation was that opposition players would hate him after losing.

Following the collapse of the XFL, Smart headed to the NFL, playing first with the Philadelphia Eagles in the fall of 2001, then signing with the Carolina Panthers the following season. After four years in Carolina, Smart signed with the Oakland Raiders in 2006, but failed to make the team's roster.

Who was responsible for the XFL?

Believing that he had the magic formula for sports success, Vince McMahon, owner of the World Wrestling Federation (now known as World Wrestling Entertainment) attempted to branch out into other sports. Failed efforts at hockey promotion in the early 1980s and a World Bodybuilding Federation in the 1990s left him undaunted, and he joined forces with NBC television to create the XFL.

The XFL emphasized rough play, trash talking, and wild antics — the same sort of entertainment that made the WWF/WWE a major force in wrestling.

Football fans were, for the most part, not amused, and the XFL lasted only one season.

Quickies

Did you know ...

- That Super Dave Osborne was part of the broadcast team for the XFL's Los Angeles Xtreme?
- That initially XFL teams could not kick for an extra point after a touchdown — they had to run or pass for that point?
- That XFL defensive backs were allowed to contact receivers at any time before the quarterback released the ball, provided that they only hit them from the side?
- The XFL's championship game was originally to be called "The Big Game at the End of the Season," but was renamed "The Million Dollar Game" because $1,000,000 was to be awarded to the winning team?

Who won the most WLAF championships?

In 1991, the World League of American Football was launched as an international spinoff of the NFL, with the intent of growing the sport on a global scale. The original league only lasted two seasons, but was revived in 1995 as the World League, later changing its name again to NFL Europe. The championship, known as the World Bowl, was contested 15 times. The Frankfurt Galaxy claimed the most trophies with four.

Quickies
Did you know ...
- That between 1998 and 2004, every single World Bowl (WLAF/NFL Europe) was won by a team from Germany?

Who was the first player selected when the NFL drafted ex-USFLers?

With the future of the USFL uncertain (or, perhaps, too certain) the NFL wanted to avoid bidding wars for ex-USFLers seeking new homes. To that end, they held a supplemental draft of USFL and CFL players.

The Tampa Bay Buccaneers had the first pick, and selected Steve Young from the Los Angeles Express. Young went on to play two seasons with the Bucs before being traded to the San Francisco 49ers. In San Francisco he served as backup to legendary quarterback Joe Montana until an injury forced Montana out of action for more than a year. Young stepped up and established himself as the team's starting quarterback, going on to win two league MVPs and one Super Bowl MVP, while Montana, after a brief return to the Niners, finished his career in Kansas City.

What Heisman Trophy winners played in the USFL?

In 1983 the upstart USFL wanted to make a splash as a serious contender to the NFL. While the L.A. Express were unable to sign Dan Marino after selecting him in the initial draft, the New Jersey Generals made up for that failure by signing the previous year's Heisman Trophy winner,

Herschel Walker. Walker left the University of Georgia a year early to be part of the new league.

The next year, another Heisman winner disappointed NFL suitors when Mike Rozier signed with the Pittsburgh Maulers (later moving to the Jacksonville Bulls after the Maulers folded after one season).

Finally, in 1985, Doug Flutie converted his Heisman win into a USFL contract when he joined Walker with the New Jersey Generals, giving the USFL their third straight Heisman winner.

The apparent coups did little for the league, which folded the next year. While Rozier's professional career was unspectacular, Walker went on to a successful NFL career while Flutie became a legend in the CFL.

What celebrity billionaire was part owner of the USFL's New Jersey Generals?

The New Jersey Generals, while lacklustre on the field, grabbed headlines in their brief existence by signing high-profile players like Heisman-winners Herschel Walker and Doug Flutie.

It's no surprise, then, that the Generals' ownership group included a man known for spending and grabbing attention: Donald Trump.

How many USFL teams played in the same cities as NFL teams?

The USFL began as a spring football league intended to exist alongside the NFL, but they showed no fear of entering NFL markets with their new product. While there were a number of franchise movements, during the course of the USFL's brief history, a total of 12 teams played in markets that had existing NFL teams. Those USFL teams were based in Boston (sharing a market with the New England Patriots), Chicago, Denver, Houston, Los Angeles, Michigan (Detroit), New Jersey (playing out of Giants Stadium), New Orleans, Philadelphia, Pittsburgh, Tampa Bay, and Washington, D.C.

In addition, the USFL looked to capture the hearts of fans whose cities had been abandoned by the NFL, placing teams in Baltimore and Oakland.

Other markets that would become future homes of NFL teams also got a taste of professional football with USFL franchises in Arizona (Phoenix), Jacksonville, Memphis, and Orlando.

> **Quickies**
> *Did you know ...*
> - A new United States Football League is planning to take the field in 2010. Like the original USFL, the new league is planned as a spring football league.

How many WLAF teams played in the same city as NFL or CFL teams?

Unlike the USFL, the World League of American Football was begun with NFL support, and did not attempt to undermine markets of existing NFL teams.

Nevertheless, one early franchise did exist in a market that already had two professional football teams. The New York/New Jersey Knights shared a market — and a stadium — with the NFL's New York Giants and Jets.

No WLAF teams took the field in CFL cities, though the Montreal Machine filled the vacancy left after the folding of the Montreal Alouettes.

Who was the first former USFL player elected to the Pro Football Hall of Fame?

He was one of the greats of the short-lived USFL, winning league-MVP honours in 1984, but Jim Kelly achieved his greatest fame as a member of the NFL's Buffalo Bills.

Kelly had spent two years with the USFL's Houston Gamblers and was slated to be the starting quarterback

> **Quickies**
> *Did you know ...*
> - That NFL Europe changed its name to NFL Europa in 2006, as all six remaining teams in the league were in Germany and the Netherlands?
> - That NFL Europe introduced a rule that awarded four points for field goals longer than 50 yards?

for the New Jersey Generals when the league folded. Kelly soon hooked up with the Bills, and went on to lead them to five division championships, and four straight Super Bowl appearances. Although Kelly's Bills are best known for their failure to win the grand prize, Kelly established himself as a legend of the game, and was inducted into the Pro Football Hall of Fame in 2002 — the first former USFL player to receive that honour.

What players won MVP awards in the USFL?

In its three-year history, the USFL had a different MVP in each season. Kelvin Bryant was the first USFL MVP in 1983, as a member of the Philadelphia Stars. Jim Kelly of the Houston Gamblers claimed the honour in 1984. Herschel Walker of the New Jersey Generals was the last league MVP in 1984.

Kelly and Walker went on to successful NFL careers, while Bryant played in the NFL, but had his career cut short by injuries.

What city has had franchises in six different professional football league — none of which were the NFL or AFL?

There's a hunger for professional football in Birmingham, Alabama, but that hunger has never translated into a team in the biggest league in the United States. The city has, however, managed to have franchises in just about every other professional football league — an achievement unmatched by any other city. There have been six professional football franchises in Birmingham:

- Birmingham Americans/Vulcans (WFL)
- Birmingham Stallions (USFL)
- Birmingham Fire (WLAF)
- Birmingham Barracudas (CFL)

- Alabama Steeldogs (af2 — the Arena Football League's developmental league)
- Birmingham Bolts (XFL)

What is the Lingerie Football League?

The most improbable league ever to emerge may be the Lingerie Football League. The idea began as a single pay-per-view event, the Lingerie Bowl, which aired opposite the Super Bowl halftime show in 2003. Two female teams played on a 50-yard field, but the outcome wasn't the draw: the women were wearing helmets, shoulder pads, and underwear. And that's it.

The idea was so successful that it was repeated the following two years, and by 2005 organizers had decided to go beyond a single game and form an actual league. Originally the league consisted of only four teams, but has since expanded to 10, with plans for future expansion.

What quarterback was a first-round draft pick in the NFL, but elected to play in the USFL instead?

In a surprising career move, the Buffalo Bills' top pick in the 1983 draft, Jim Kelly, decided that the USFL was the place to be. Kelly cited cold weather and poor attendance as reasons for snubbing the Bills. However, the Bills retained rights to Kelly, and when the USFL folded in 1986, Kelly joined the team and became one of the city's most accomplished and popular athletes.

Who won the last game in USFL history?

The final game in USFL history was the 1985 championship game. For a league that had struggled to gain acceptance, the curtain-closer was an exciting contest, held at Giants Stadium in East Rutherford, New

Jersey. With the Baltimore Stars leading 28–24 in the dying minutes of the game, the Oakland Invaders mounted a drive from deep in their own end and looked poised to take the lead. Then fullback Tom Newton was penalized for unnecessary roughness, killing the drive and handing the win to the Stars.

What was the "Action Point"?

The World Football League introduced some novel rules. One of them was the Action Point. The WFL increased the value of an unconverted touchdown to seven points, and gave teams a chance at an eight point through a convert. But that convert couldn't be attained by kicking; teams had to run or pass for the "Action Point."

How many non-U.S. teams were part of the World Football League?

The World Football League was a failed attempt to provide competition for the National Football League.

League founder Gary Davidson, who also had the dubious distinction of helping to launch the World Hockey Association and the American Basketball Association, had ambitious plans to make the new football league a global one.

Unfortunately, attempts to deliver non-American entries were fruitless. The Toronto Northmen were to be the league's lone Canadian representative until Prime Minister Pierre Trudeau attempted to block the move with the Canada Football Act, which was designed to prevent foreign leagues from competing with the Canadian Football League on

Canadian soil.

Though the proposed act was never passed into law, the threat was sufficient to cause the Northmen to change homes, becoming the Memphis Southmen.

No international teams played in the WFL, which folded in 1975, partway through its second season.

Who won the last World Football League Championship?

The World Football League was a disaster. While it impressed observers with average attendances of well over 40,000 at the beginning of its inaugural season in 1974, it was soon discovered that the overwhelming majority of those spectators were given free tickets. Attendance was low, interest was low, and many were surprised when the league announced it would return for year two.

The second season was a mistake, and teams began folding partway through the season. With the writing on the wall, the league as a whole folded, and awarded their second and last championship to the Birmingham Vulcans, who happened to have the league's best record at the time of dissolution.

Quickies

Did you know ...

- That it was the World Football League that prompted the NFL to move its goal posts? The NFL had had goal posts on the goal line for years. When the WFL came around, their goal posts were at the back of the end zone. Nervous that players might prefer the safety of the new league, but more importantly that fans might like how this and other rule differences opened up the field for the offence, the NFL decided to move their goal posts to the back of the end zone.

Which USFL team featured two 100-catch receivers in the same season?

The Houston Gamblers got off to a quick start in their USFL existence, finishing with a 13–5 regular-season record. Though they were ousted in the first round of the playoffs, the team did make history

Quickies

Did you know ...

- That the MVP of the WFL's World Bowl Championship Game received a cash prize? The money was stacked on a table at midfield after the game.

that season, becoming the first team in professional football history to boast two receivers with more than 100 catches in the same years. Richard Johnson had 115 catches, while Ricky Sanders had 101.

How many countries had teams in the World League of American Football?

At its inception in 1991, the World League of American Football had the international flavour its name suggested, with teams based in five different nations: England (London Monarchs), Spain (Barcelona Dragons), Germany (Frankfurt Galaxy), Canada (Montreal Machine), and the United States (six teams).

The league suspended operations after the 1992 season, but re-emerged in 1995, as an all-European league, adding teams in Scotland and the Netherlands, as well as a second team in Germany.

Ultimately the league morphed into NFL Europe and continued for several seasons until folding in 2007.

Who won the first WLAF championship?

The three European teams in the first season of the World League of American Football dominated their North American counterparts. No North American team had a winning record, while the London Monarchs finished 9–1–0, the Barcelona Dragons 8–2–0, and the Frankfurt Galaxy 7–3–0. This was just fine with the European fans, who were the only ones supporting the league in large numbers.

The league's first championship game, World Bowl I, pitted London against Barcelona. The Monarchs dominated, winning 21–0. Safety Dan Crossman was the first and only defensive player to be named World Bowl MVP.

Who came up with the idea of arena football?

While attending a Major Indoor Soccer League game at Madison Square Garden in 1981, Jim Foster — a former NFL and future USFL executive — found inspiration. If one brand of "football" could be moved indoors and onto a smaller field, why not American football?

He jotted down some ideas, including such off-beat concepts as the rebound nets at the back of the end zones. Then, while he worked with the USFL, he put the idea on hold. When the USFL folded, he returned to his dream and set about starting a league. By 1987, he'd found investors and host cities and launched the Arena Football League. Foster was the league's first commissioner, and later became owner of the Iowa Barnstormers.

The league had only novelty appeal at first, but eventually built up a large enough fan base to maintain itself until 2008 before electing to take the 2009 season off due to financial circumstances. The AFL plans to return in 2010.

Quickies
Did you know ...
- That Arena Football League founder Jim Foster was actually prepared to launch his new league in 1983? He chose not to proceed due to the creation of the USFL.

What teams played the first arena football game?

The first arena football game was a "play-test" game. When Jim Foster was looking to take his idea for arena football and turn it into an actual league, he decided to test his rules in actual competition. He assembled two teams of semi-pro and former college players, and played a game in Rockford, Illinois in 1986. He named the teams the Rockford Metros and the Chicago Politicians. Rockford won the game, 30–18.

A year later, the first official Arena Football League game was played. The

Quickies
Did you know ...
- That there were only four teams in the Arena Football League's first season? (Chicago Bruisers, Denver Dynamite, Pittsburgh Gladiators, and Washington Commandos.)
- That the rules and equipment used by the Arena Football League were protected by a patent until 2007?
- That the Detroit Drive played in every single ArenaBowl from the league's founding in 1988 until they moved to Massachusetts in 1994?
- That the Arena Football League plans to resume play in 2010?

137

Washington Commandos defeated the Pittsburgh Gladiators 48–46.

Which rock star is co-owner of an Arena Football League team?

When the Arena Football League expanded in 2003, it added a high-profile owner to the league. Jon Bon Jovi, who achieved fame through his solo work and his band Bon Jovi, became co-owner of the Philadelphia Soul, along with his partner, real-estate developer Craig Spencer.

Who founded the All-America Football Conference?

The AAFC was an influential upstart league that played from 1946 to 1949. It was founded by Arch Ward, a sports editor with the *Chicago Tribune*. In addition to founding the AAFC, he also created the Golden Gloves boxing tournament and the Major League Baseball All-Star Game.

Which AAFC teams joined the NFL?

When the All-America Football Conference merged with the National Football League in 1946, three teams survived: the Baltimore Colts, the Cleveland Browns, and the San Francisco 49ers. The Colts folded after the 1950 season, and were replaced by a new Baltimore Colts team in 1953.

the
fab forty:
the greatest
plays in football

1. Eli Manning to David Tyree, Super Bowl XLII

Sorry, Steelers and Niners fans, but nothing in Super Bowl lore compares to this incredible play that had greatness on both ends.

The New England Patriots were on the verge of the second perfect season in NFL history. With 1:15 remaining, they had the underdog New York Giants on the ropes, facing a third-and-five situation from their own 44-yard line. Giants quarterback Eli Manning took the snap, but immediately faced pressure. On the verge of being sacked, he escaped the grasp of a Patriots defender and hurled the ball deep into Patriots territory.

David Tyree, at the Pats' 24-yard line, was covered by safety Rodney Harrison, but leapt over the defender to reach the ball. Only able to keep one hand on the ball, he held the pigskin against his helmet, holding on until he was able to wrap a second hand around it as he hit the ground.

The miracle pass and catch led to a Super Bowl-winning touchdown as the Giants pulled off one of the biggest upsets in memory.

2. Santonio Holmes, Super Bowl XLIII

The Pittsburgh Steelers regained their position as the winningest team in Super Bowl history on one of the greatest catches the championship game has seen.

In the 2009 game, the Arizona Cardinals had come back from a 20–7 deficit to take a 20–23 lead with just over two minutes left. The Steelers, starting from their own 22-yard line, brought the ball to the Cardinals' six, thanks to a passing play to Santonio Holmes. But Holmes would not stop there.

On second and goal, quarterback Ben Roethlisberger sailed a pass to the right back corner of the end zone. A leaping Holmes snagged the ball in the air, then, as he came down, managed to get the toes of both feet in bounds, and gained control of the ball before hitting the ground.

Many fans will consider it sacrilege to place any catch above "The Catch" of Dwight Clark, but the rationale is simple: bigger game, tougher catch.

3. The Immaculate Reception —
Terry Bradshaw to Franco Harris

The 1972 AFC divisional playoff game between the Pittsburgh Steelers and the Oakland Raiders came down to the last minute. Trailing 7–6 with only 22 seconds to play, the Steelers were facing fourth and 10 from their own 40. Quarterback Terry Bradshaw was unable to find his intended receiver, Barry Pearson, and looked to John Fuqua. Bradshaw released the throw, but Fuqua was hit by safety Jack Tatum as the ball arrived, and the ball apparently bounced off of Tatum.

Steelers running back Franco Harris was in the area and was able to catch the ball before it hit the ground. Harris took the ball into the end zone for the game-winning score.

The play was controversial: the Raiders argued that the ball bounced off Fuqua, not Tatum, and therefore, according to NFL rules at the time, the pass should have been ruled incomplete. (A ball could not be touched by two offensive players in succession.) The officials ruled with the Steelers.

4. The Catch — Joe Montana to Dwight Clark

A masterful drive put the San Francisco 49ers deep in Dallas Cowboys territory in the fourth quarter of the 1982 NFC Championship Game, and they found themselves on the six-yard line. But with Dallas leading 27–21, the Niners needed a touchdown. On third down, with 58 seconds remaining, quarterback Joe Montana ran a Sprint Right Option that was intended to find Freddie Solomon. Solomon was covered, however, and Montana, pursued by three Cowboys, threw up a prayer in the direction of Dwight Clark, who was at the back of the end zone. Clark leapt, made a fingertip catch, and the 49ers squeaked past the Cowboys to win the NFC title. They went on to win the Super Bowl.

5. Doug Flutie to Gerard Phelan, 1984

This was the Hail Mary pass that may have surpassed the original Roger Staubach Hail Mary pass. Doug Flutie was a well-known player and Heisman Trophy candidate before this play, but became a household name afterward, particularly in New England.

The highly anticipated game pitted Flutie's Boston College against Bernie Kosar's University of Miami, and it looked as though the role of hero belonged to Kosar when he shepherded his team to a touchdown in the final minute to take a 45–41 lead. But Flutie's desperation throw from his own 36-yard line found Gerry Phelan in the end zone for the game-winning score on the final play of the game, cementing his reputation and cinching the Heisman.

6. Alan Ameche, 1958 NFL Championship

The 1958 NFL Championship Game between the New York Giants and the Baltimore Colts has often been called the greatest game ever played, and many credit the contest with helping to create an explosion of interest in the National Football League. The game featured 12 future Hall of Famers.

The back and forth contact saw big-play passing (including an 86-yard gain on a pass from Giants quarterback Charlier Conerly to Kyle Rote) and clutch drives (Johnny Unitas led the Colts from their own 11-yard line to set up a game tying field goal with seven seconds remaining).

In overtime, the Colts marched the ball from their own 19-yard line and, from the Giants' one, Alan Ameche took the hand-off into the end zone for the win. While the play itself was only a one-yard run, it punctuated a fantastic drive at the end of a monumental game.

7. Tom Clements to Tony Gabriel, 1976 Grey Cup

This battle between the two Riders teams also pitted two future Hall of Fame quarterbacks against each other: the Saskatchewan Roughriders'

Ron Lancaster, and the Ottawa Rough Riders' Tom Clements. But late in the game it looked like the Saskatchewan defence might be the stars of the game, as a goal line stand forced Ottawa to turn the ball over on downs with less than two minutes to play and Saskatchewan ahead, 20–16.

Then, it was Ottawa's turn to come up big as they got the ball back into the hands of Clements. With 20 seconds to play, Clements sent Gabriel long. Gabriel faked a post pattern then ran toward the corner of the end zone where Clements hit him with a 24-yard touchdown pass to win the Cup.

8. The Play — University of California, 1982

The end of this annual Big Game between Cal and Stanford is remembered not just because it was dramatic, but because it was bizarre. After John Elway led the Stanford squad from deep in their own end to a field goal kick by Mark Harmon with four seconds remaining, it was going to take a miracle for Cal to win. And a miracle is what occurred.

Harmon's kickoff after the field goal was a squib kick that was picked up by Kevin Moen. Moen pitched to Richard Rodgers, and Rodgers lateralled to Dwight Garner. Garner was surrounded by Stanford players and appeared to be on his way to the turf. In fact, the Stanford marching band thought he *was* down and began to take the field.

But the play was still live. Garner tossed the ball to Mariet Ford, and Ford, who by this time was dodging members of the Stanford team *and* the Stanford band, threw the ball blindly behind him as he was falling to the turf. The ball was caught by Moen who found a route through the marching band and into the end zone.

9. The Tackle — Mike Jones, Super Bowl XXXIV

Defensive plays rarely get their due in discussions of great plays, but the final moment of Super Bowl XXXIV became one of the most talked-about stops in the game's history.

In the third quarter, the Tennessee Titans trailed the St. Louis Rams 16–0, but they stormed back to tie the game 16–16 late in the game. The Rams then answered with a touchdown on a 76-yard play.

The Titans had one last drive to tie the game. Starting from their own 10-yard line, the odds looked long, but their drive took them 80 yards to the Rams' 10.

With six second remaining, Titans quarterback Steve McNair threw to an open Mike Dyson at the five-yard line. Mike Jones, who had been covering another player, spotted the play, turned, and wrapped his arms around Dyson's legs after he received the ball. He brought Dyson down at the one-yard line as time expired and Dyson reached in vain for the goal line.

10. Eli Manning to Plaxico Burress, Super Bowl XLII

Though it was almost an anticlimax after the heroic catch by David Tyree that preceded it, Burress's touchdown capped off one of the most exciting drives, and exciting games, in Super Bowl memory.

Trailing 14–10 with 39 seconds remaining, the New York Giants needed a touchdown to knock of the heavily favoured New England Patriots. (The Patriots, for their part, were on the verge of a perfect season.) As Eli Manning took the snap at the 12-yard line, Plaxico Burress ran straight for the back corner of the end zone. Manning threw the ball toward Burress, who was wide open. As scripted, Burress turned toward the throw at the last second, and caught the Super Bowl-winner.

11. The Bluegrass Miracle — Marcus Randall to Devery Henderson, 2002

The LSU Tigers had a commanding 14-point lead in their game against the Kentucky Wildcats, but the underdog Kentucky team, playing on home turf, was not going to be defeated easily. A fourth-quarter comeback was capped by a Taylor Begley field goal to give the Wildcats a 30–27 lead with 11 seconds remaining. After the kickoff and a play by LSU, there were two seconds left, and the ball was deep in LSU's end.

The Wildcats gave their coach a Gatorade shower and the fans prepared to storm the field to celebrate the upset win. But LSU quarterback Marcus Randall took the snap on the last play of the game and, from his own 18-yard line, threw to Devery Henderson, who was surrounded by Wildcat players at the Kentucky 18. Henderson ran the rest of the way to give the Tigers a 33–30 win.

Many Kentucky fans had not seen the catch and touchdown, and were celebrating a "win" by tearing down the goal posts, only to be devastated as news spread of what came to be known as "The Bluegrass Miracle."

12. The Ice Bowl — Bart Starr, 1967 NFL Championship

On a frozen field in Green Bay, with the weather so cold that the referees could not use their whistles, the Packers and the Dallas Cowboys played a true classic. After building up a 14–0 lead, the Packers saw the Cowboys storm back with 17 unanswered points, thanks in large part to two costly Green Bay fumbles.

With 16 seconds to play, Green Bay was third-and-goal from the Cowboys' three-yard line. Many expected a passing play, since a run stopped short of the goal line would likely result in time expiring. Instead, Starr called his own number, running a quarterback sneak that scored the touchdown as the Packers won their third straight NFL Championship.

13. The Hail Mary Pass — Roger Staubach, 1975 NFC Divisional Playoff

This was the play that gave rise to the term "Hail Mary pass."

The Dallas Cowboys trailed the Minnesota Vikings 14–10 with 24 seconds remaining, and had the ball at midfield. Working from the shotgun, Staubach sent Drew Pearson long, took the snap, and released the ball from his own 40-yard line. The ball travelled 55 yards in the air, finding Pearson at the five, and from there he took the ball into the end zone.

14. Ken Ploen, 1961 Grey Cup

Grey Cups have a history of being tight contests, but the 1961 final was unique in that it went into overtime, and has been called one of the greatest Grey Cups ever played.

Ken Ploen, in his fifth year as a quarterback with the Winnipeg Blue Bombers, was midway through a Hall of Fame career when he pulled off one of the most memorable touchdown runs in the championship's history. With just over six minutes to play in overtime, he called his own number and scampered around a host of Hamilton Tiger-Cat defenders for an 18-yard touchdown run that lifted the Bombers to their third Grey Cup in four years.

15. The Music City Miracle — Lorenzo Neal to Frank Wycheck to Kevin Dyson, 2000 AFC Wildcard

It was to be Wade Phillips' vindication. The Buffalo Bills coach had been heavily criticized for inexplicably electing to start quarterback Rob Johnson in the AFC Wildcard Game instead of Doug Flutie, who had led the team into the playoffs, starting 15 games that season. After falling behind 12–0 at the half, it looked like Phillips would have egg on his face, but the Bills fought back and, with 16 seconds remaining, took a 16–15 lead on a 41-yard field goal by Steve Christie. Bills fans were revelling, and Phillips was ready to say his told-ya-so's.

But the Tennessee Titans had other ideas, and brought out a trick play that they'd been rehearsing in practice. The kickoff was received by Lorenzo Neal at the Titans' 25-yard line. Neal handed off to Frank Wycheck, and Wycheck threw a lateral pass to Kevin Dyson, who evaded all Bills defenders and ran the ball into the end zone for a miraculous game-winning touchdown.

16. Hook and Lateral — Strock to Harris to Nathan, 1982 AFC Divisional Playoff

In this fantastic playoff game, the Miami Dolphins pulled off a play that is noteworthy not for its impact on the outcome of the game, but for its sheer brilliance and perfect execution.

The Dolphins had been trailing 24–0, but scored 10 points and had the ball on the San Diego Chargers' 40-yard line with one chance to make a play before halftime. The Fins called a timeout, and quarterback Don Strock got instructions from coach Don Shula on the sideline. The call was a trick play: a hook and lateral.

Strock threw the ball to Duriel Harris at the Chargers' 25, and Harris immediately lateralled back to running back Tony Nathan, who ran into the end zone to close the gap to 24–17.

The game ultimately went into overtime and the Chargers won, but the Dolphins' masterful hook and lateral play arguably stole the show.

17. Joe Montana to John Taylor, Super Bowl XXIII

Joe Montana already had a reputation as a clutch quarterback coming into the 1989 Super Bowl, but he cemented that reputation in the final minutes of the game.

The San Francisco 49ers trailed the Cincinnati Bengals 16–13 and were pinned deep in their own end. Montana then led a drive downfield that put the Niners on the Bengals' 10-yard line. With 39 seconds to play, most — including the Bengals — were expecting Montana to seek out legendary receiver Jerry Rice. Instead, he targeted John Taylor, and threaded a pass between two Bengals receivers that hit Taylor on the numbers to win the game.

18. Vic Washington, 1968 Grey Cup

With the Ottawa Rough Riders trailing the Calgary Stampeders 14–10 in the fourth quarter, Ottawa was looking to gain some ground. The play that turned things around for them was nearly a disaster.

Running back Vic Washington took the handoff and had a free route down the sideline, but, worried about his footing (the ground was muddy), he fumbled the ball. Fortunately for Washington, the fumble bounced back into his hands and he completed his touchdown run — a 79-yard run from scrimmage that remains a Grey Cup record.

After this play, the teams exchanged touchdowns and Ottawa won the game, 24–21.

19. John Riggins, Super Bowl XVII

It was the fourth quarter, and the Redskins, trailing by four, elected to gamble on fourth and one. Hall of Fame quarterback Joe Theisman handed off to John Riggins, who broke a tackle and then had a free route to the end zone for a 43-yard touchdown. The Skins went up 20–17, then added another touchdown to win the title.

20. Anthony Calvillo to Pat Woodcock, 2002 Grey Cup

The Montreal Alouettes had won a Grey Cup in 1995, but they were playing in Baltimore at the time. The city of Montreal had not won the championship since 1977.

In the second quarter the Als made a statement with the longest touchdown reception in Grey Cup history. Anthony Calvillo, at his own 11, took the snap and found a wide-open Pat Woodcock at the 40. Woodcock eluded the grasp of an Edmonton defender and ran 70 more yards for the touchdown — a total of 99 yards on the play.

The Alouettes went on to win the game, 26–16.

21. San Francisco 49ers Defence, Super Bowl XVI

It may have been the greatest goal line stand in football history. It was certainly the most timely.

The Cincinnati Bengals were trailing 20–7 late in the third quarter, but were charging. They marched the ball deep into San Francisco territory and were first and goal from the three. A score seemed inevitable, but the 49ers defence stopped the Bengals at the one on three consecutive plays. The Bengals gambled on fourth down instead of kicking the field goal. Pete Johnson took the handoff and tried to penetrate the Niners' defence, by defenders Jack Reynolds, Ronnie Lott, and Dan Bunz stopped him short of the goal line to take over on downs.

Though the Bengals outscored the 49ers 14–6 in the fourth quarter, the goal line stand proved pivotal as San Francisco held on for a 26–21 win.

22. John Elway to Mark Jackson,
1987 AFC Championship

Some plays are great on their own, while others are great in context. The touchdown pass from John Elway to Mark Jackson with 37 seconds left in the 1987 AFC Championship game was dramatic — it tied the game, allowing the Broncos to beat the Cleveland Browns in overtime — but it was the culmination of a series of plays. The Broncos had started on their own two-yard line, but led by a gutsy John Elway, they ate up more than five minutes of time on a 15-play, 98-yard march that is known in football lore as "The Drive."

23. The Goal Line Stand — Alabama defence,
1979 Sugar Bowl

In the pre-BCS days of college football, it was rare for the number one and number two teams to meet head to head in a bowl game, but that's what happened when Alabama took on Penn State in the 1979 Sugar Bowl.

The defensive tussle was tight throughout the game, and Alabama led 14–7 late in the fourth quarter when Penn State forced a turnover on the 'Bama 19. Penn State made another first down and were first and goal from the eight-yard line.

The Alabama defence gave, but wouldn't break as, after three plays, Penn State was able to advance to less than a yard from the end zone, but were unable to break the plane of the goal line. On fourth and inches, ball-carrier Mike Guman attempted to find a hole in the line, but was met by Murray Legg and Barry Krauss. Krauss was knocked unconscious on the play, but Guman and Penn State were kept out of the end zone, and Alabama held on to win the game, and the National Championship.

24. Norm Van Brocklin, 1951 NFL Championship

The battle for the 1951 NFL crown came down to a dramatic last quarter. The Los Angeles Rams went up 17–10 on a field goal early in the quarter, but the Cleveland Browns hung tough. They culminated a 70-yard drive, with a five-yard touchdown run by fullback Ken Carpenter midway through the quarter to tie the game.

But the Rams answered right away. Starting from his own 27-yard line, quarterback Norm Van Brocklin hit Tom Fears at midfield, and the wide receiver took the ball all the way to the end zone for a 24–17 lead. The Rams held on to win the title.

25. Kordell Stewart, 1994

Stewart and the University of Colorado Buffaloes scored two touchdowns in just over two minutes to win their September 24 matchup against Michigan, but it was the drama of the second touchdown that has become one of the quarterback's most enduring memories.

Down 26–21 on the last play of the game, Kordell sailed a Hail Mary pass from his own 35 into a sea of players in the Michigan end zone. The ball found the hands of Michael Westbrook as Colorado won the game, 27–26.

26. Jared Zabransky, 2007 Fiesta Bowl

Zabransky actually gets credit for two plays in this game. Facing fourth and long from midfield with 19 seconds remaining, Zabransky and Boise State ran a hook and lateral — Zabransky passed to Drisan James, James lateralled to Jerard Rabb, and Rabb went to the end zone to tie Oklahoma and send the game to overtime.

In overtime, Boise State was trailing by seven when they scored a touchdown. They then elected to attempt to win the game with a two-point conversion. They used another trick play — the Statue of Liberty play. Zabransky faked the throw and handed off to Ian Johnson, who scored the conversion as Boise State upset the Oklahoma Sooners 43–42 in one of the greatest college football games ever played.

27. Desmond Howard, Super Bowl XXXI

The 1997 Super Bowl was a tight battle until late in the third quarter. The New England Patriots had just scored to move within six points of the Green Bay Packers.

The ensuing kickoff was deep — it was caught by Desmond Howard at his own one-yard line. But that was the high-water mark for the Patriots in this game, because after making the catch, Howard ran the ball 99 yards, virtually straight up the middle (he was only touched once) for a touchdown that sucked the life out of New England. To add insult to injury, the Packers completed a two-point conversion to go up 35–21 — a score that would stand through the fourth quarter.

Howard became the first special-teams player to be named Super Bowl MVP.

28. Fumblerooskie — Dean Steinkuhler, 1984 Orange Bowl

It's tough not to love a great trick play when it's perfectly executed, particular when it comes in a great game. The Nebraska Cornhuskers were trailing the Miami Hurricans 17–0, and were desperate to get back in the game. They went to a trick play they'd rehearsed in practice — the fumblerooskie. Quarterback Turner Gill purposely let the snap hit his hands and drop to the turf, then rolled back and to his right. Lineman Dean Steinkuhler picked up the ball and ran to the left, taking the ball in for a touchdown from the 20-yard line to get Nebraska back in the game.

The Huskers ended up losing, 31–30, in one of the best Orange Bowls ever played, but the fumblerooskie remains the most memorable moment of the game.

29. Henry "Gizmo" Williams, 1987 Grey Cup

The Edmonton Eskimos won the 1987 Grey Cup over the Toronto Argonauts on a last-second field goal by Jerry Kauric, but the most spectacular play of the game came in the first quarter. Argos kicker Lance Chomyc missed on a field goal attempt, which was caught by Gizmo Williams five yards deep in the end zone. Williams brought the ball out, dodged Argos tacklers, headed to the sidelines, and turned upfield. He was untouched the rest of the way as he completed a Grey Cup-record 115-yard return for a touchdown. The Eskimos won the game 38–36 and Damon Allen was named MVP, but Williams' run was the highlight that endured.

30. Adam Vinatieri, Super Bowl XXXVI

Kickers rarely get props for their game-winning heroics, but when one kicker wins two Super Bowls with field goals, it's only fair that at least one of those makes a "greatest plays" list.

The Los Angeles Rams had tied the 2002 Super Bowl with 1:30 remaining. At the time, it looked like the heroics of Kurt Warner would be the story of the game. But Patriots quarterback Tom Brady used six plays — all passes — to get the ball across midfield to set up a field-goal try. As the clock expired, Adam Vinatieri nailed a 48-yard field goal straight through the centre of the uprights. It was the first time a Super Bowl had been won with a score on the final play of the game.

Two years later Vinatieri repeated his heroics, kicking a 41-yard field goal with six seconds remaining to help the Patriots to another Super Bowl win.

31. Marcus Allen, Super Bowl XVIII

The 1984 Super Bowl was a blowout, but the performance of Marcus Allen made it memorable. En route to winning the MVP, he ran for 191 yards (a record at the time) and two touchdowns. But the highlight of the game was a 74-yard touchdown run from scrimmage — a record that would stand for 22 years.

Allen took the handoff from L.A. Raiders quarterback Jim Plunkett and ran to the left, but reversed field when confronted by a Redskins defender. He then turned upfield and scampered to the end zone to put the Raiders up 35–9. They'd add a field goal in the fourth quarter to complete the thrashing.

32. Lynn Swann, Super Bowl X

It's a shame that one of the greatest catches in Super Bowl history — Lynn Swann's magnificent grab in the 1976 contest — didn't actually lead to a score, but it was a catch that would remain on Swann highlight reels in perpetuity.

The play came in the second quarter, with the Steelers pinned deep in their own end. Scrimmaging from their own six-yard line, Terry Bradshaw rolled back to the goal line and threw the ball 50 feet in the air. Swann, covered by Mark Washington, leapt, tipped the ball in the air, then caught the ball and brought it to the Cowboys' 37.

33. James Harrison, Super Bowl XLIII

One of two entries from the 2009 championship, the touchdown by James Harrison was a huge turning point in the game.

The Arizona Cardinals were threatening. Trailing 10–7, they were on the Steelers' two-yard line with 18 seconds to go in the first half, and a sterling opportunity take a lead into the half. But Kurt Warner's touchdown pass found the wrong-coloured jersey. Linebacker James Harrison picked off the pass on the goal line and returned it 100 yards for a touchdown — the longest interception return in Super Bowl history.

34. Kellen Winslow, 1982 AFC Divisional Playoff

The 1982 playoff game that came to be known as "The Epic in Miami" may have gone down as a great comeback win for the Miami Dolphins, if not for the heroic performance of Sand Diego Chargers tight end Kellen Winslow.

Winslow caught 13 passes for 166 yards, scoring one touchdown, but it was a play on defence that saved the day for the Chargers. He blocked a 43-yard field goal attempt that would have won the game for Miami. Instead, the Chargers went on to win in overtime.

Winslow's performance that day was all the more impressive given that he was suffering from cramping and dehydration and had to be treated for a pinched nerve during the game. After the game ended, he needed to be helped to the locker room by his teammates.

35. George Blanda to Billy Cannon, 1960 AFL Championship

Played on New Year's Day 1961, the 1960 AFL Championship Game was a tight affair that came down to the wire. But the key play that helped the Houston Oilers to defeat the Los Angeles Chargers came in the second quarter, when Oilers quarterback George Blanda tossed a short pass to

Billy Cannon, who broke a tackle and ran all the way for an 88-yard touchdown. The Oilers went on to win the game, 24–16.

36. The Hidden-Ball Trick, 1902

Legendary coach Pop Warner debuted one of the most famous football gag plays in a 1902 game between his Carlisle Indians and Harvard. The hidden-ball trick calls for a player to hide the ball inside his clothing while the opposing team assumes another player is the ball-carrier. Warner wasn't content to trust standard jerseys, though. He had jerseys specially made with elastic bands at the waist to ensure the ball stayed in.

As Carlisle received the ball to start the second half, quarterback Jimmie Johnson made the catch and then, after teammates huddle around to obscure the view, quickly slipped up the back of the shirt of teammate Charles Dillon. The huddle then broke and multiple players acted as if they had the ball while Dillon — the bulge of the ball obscured at his back, swung his arms freely so there could be no doubt he didn't have the ball in his hands. As Harvard players looked for the ball, Dillon ran upfield for the touchdown.

It is now illegal in virtually all leagues to hide the ball underneath clothing.

37. Eddie Brown, 1996 Grey Cup

For a play to be considered "great" when it comes in the first quarter, and is pulled off by a member of the losing team, it has to be something special. In the snowy 1996 Grey Cup, Edmonton Eskimos quarterback Danny McManus hurled a frozen football towards receiver Eddie Brown on the sidelines. The ball was just within Brown's reach, but pulling the rock-hard ball in was not going to be an easy feat. It bounced off his fingers, then off his knee, and Brown reached down to snare the ball off his shoelaces. He never broke stride, and took the ball to the end zone for a 64-yard score.

The Eskimos took a 9–0 lead on the play, but Doug Flutie and the Toronto Argonauts would go on to win the game, 43–37.

38. Deion Sanders, 1988

Deion Sanders was always considered a bit cocky, but in a 1988 college game his legs proved his mouth right. Sanders' Florida State team, ranked number 10 in the nation, was facing the number three ranked Clemson, who had a legitimate shot at a National Championship that season. In the third quarter, Florida State trailed 14–7 and Clemson was preparing to punt. Before the kick was made, Sanders turned to the Clemson bench and shouted, "This one's going back!" And it did. Sanders was barely touched as he returned the punt 76 yards for a touchdown. Florida State went on to win the game 24–21, crushing Clemson's hopes for a national title.

39. The Holy Roller — Oakland Raiders, 1978

A play that gets a name slapped on it is generally something special, but the play that came to be known as "The Holy Roller" was more controversial than great.

With 10 seconds remaining, the Oakland Raiders trailed the San Diego Chargers 14–10. They were on the Chargers' 14. Quarterback Ken Stabler looked for a receiver, but was caught by San Diego linebacker Woodrow Lowe. Unable to escape Lowe's clutches, Stabler fumbled the ball forward. Running back Pete Banaszak attempted to pick up the ball, but lost his footing and pushed the ball forward. Next, tight end Dave Casper tried but failed to pick up the ball, which went into the end zone. Casper then fell on it for a game-winning touchdown.

The controversy came when the Chargers argued that Stabler, Banaszak, and Casper purposely moved the ball forward — in each case, the act would have been illegal. But the officials sided with the Raiders, and the play stood.

40. Lewis Bennett, 1987

It might be the greatest catch that meant nothing that was ever made. In a game against the San Francisco 49ers in 1987, New York Giants wide receiver Bennett was being completely mauled by a defender. A pass from midfield was short, and Lewis needed to reach both hands around the defender to tip the ball in the air, and then he caught it for a touchdown.

Why didn't the play matter, particularly considering it came against the 49ers, a powerhouse of the 1980s? Because it was a game played by replacement players during the 1987 NFL strike. The stakes put the catch at the bottom of the list; the brilliance of the catch gets it *on* the list.

champions

Super Bowl Champions

Game	Winner	Date
I*	Green Bay Packers	January 15, 1967
II*	Green Bay Packers	January 14, 1968
III*	New York Jets	January 12, 1969
IV*	Kansas City Chiefs	January 11, 1970
V	Baltimore Colts	January 17, 1971
VI	Dallas Cowboys	January 16, 1972
VII	Miami Dolphins	January 14, 1973
VIII	Miami Dolphins	January 13, 1974
IX	Pittsburgh Steelers	January 12, 1975
X	Pittsburgh Steelers	January 18, 1976
XI	Oakland Raiders	January 9, 1977
XII	Dallas Cowboys	January 15, 1978
XIII	Pittsburgh Steelers	January 21, 1979
XIV	Pittsburgh Steelers	January 20, 1980
XV	Oakland Raiders	January 25, 1981
XVI	San Francisco 49ers	January 24, 1982
XVII	Washington Redskins	January 30, 1983
XVIII	Los Angeles Raiders	January 22, 1984
XIX	San Francisco 49ers	January 20, 1985
XX	Chicago Bears	January 26, 1986
XXI	New York Giants	January 25, 1987
XXII	Washington Redskins	January 31, 1988
XXIII	San Francisco 49ers	January 22, 1989
XXIV	San Francisco 49ers	January 28, 1990
XXV	New York Giants	January 27, 1991
XXVI	Washington Redskins	January 26, 1992
XXVII	Dallas Cowboys	January 31, 1993
XXVIII	Dallas Cowboys	January 30, 1994
XXIX	San Francisco 49ers	January 29, 1995

XXX	Dallas Cowboys	January 28, 1996
XXXI	Green Bay Packers	January 26, 1997
XXXII	Denver Broncos	January 25, 1998
XXXIII	Denver Broncos	January 31, 1999
XXXIV	St. Louis Rams	January 30, 2000
XXXV	Baltimore Ravens	January 28, 2001
XXXVI	New England Patriots	February 3, 2002
XXXVII	Tampa Bay Buccaneers	January 26, 2003
XXXVIII	New England Patriots	February 1, 2004
XXXIX	New England Patriots	February 6, 2005
XL	Pittsburgh Steelers	February 5, 2006
XLI	Indianapolis Colts	February 4, 2007
XLII	New York Giants	February 3, 2008
XLIII	Pittsburgh Steelers	February 1, 2009

* *The first four Super Bowls were called the "AFL-NFL Championship Game." The name "Super Bowl" and the corresponding Roman numeral were applied to those games retroactively.*

Great Teams:
The 1985 Chicago Bears
As improbable as it may seem, the Bears' 15–1 record does not do justice to the dominance of the team. With Walter Payton on offence and Mike Singletary on defence, the team thrashed virtually every opponent they faced in the regular season, but truly showed their dominance in the playoffs, winning 21–0 and then 24–0, finally winning the Super Bowl with a 46–10 clobbering of the New England Patriots.

National Football League Champions
(before the Super Bowl era)

Year	Winner
1920*	Akron Pros
1921*	Chicago Staleys
1922*	Canton Bulldogs
1923*	Canton Bulldogs
1924*	Cleveland Bulldogs
1925*	Chicago Cardinals
1926*	Frankford Yellow Jackets
1927*	New York Giants
1928*	Providence Steam Roller
1929*	Green Bay Packers
1930*	Green Bay Packers
1931*	Green Bay Packers
1932*	Chicago Bears
1933	Chicago Bears
1934	New York Giants
1935	Detroit Lions
1936	Green Bay Packers
1937	Washington Redskins
1938	New York Giants
1939	Green Bay Packers
1940	Chicago Bears
1941	Chicago Bears
1942	Washington Redskins
1943	Chicago Bears
1944	Green Bay Packers
1945	Cleveland Rams
1946	Chicago Bears
1947	Chicago Cardinals

1948	Philadelphia Eagles
1949	Philadelphia Eagles
1950	Cleveland Browns
1951	Los Angeles Rams
1952	Detroit Lions
1953	Detroit Lions
1954	Cleveland Browns
1955	Cleveland Browns
1956	New York Giants
1957	Detroit Lions
1958	Baltimore Colts
1959	Baltimore Colts
1960	Philadelphia Eagles
1961	Green Bay Packers
1962	Green Bay Packers
1963	Chicago Bears
1964	Cleveland Browns
1965	Green Bay Packers

* Prior to 1933, champions were determined by their regular season records. From 1933 onward, championship games were played.

Great Teams:
The 1962 Green Bay Packers

Having Vince Lombardi as head coach is always a good way to start; throw in the versatile halfback Paul Hornung, fullback John Taylor, and Hall of Fame quarterback Bart Starr and you've got the makings of one of the all-time great teams. The Packers were so dominant that in one game they compiled 628 yards on offence while holding their opponents to a mere 54 yards. And in the NFL Championship, Ray Nitschke proved that the team did not just have great offensive players, as the defensive linebacker shut down the New York Giants and was named the game's MVP.

Great Teams:
The 1989 San Fransisco 49ers
They could beat you in the air or on the ground. Quarterback Joe Montana, and receivers Jerry Rice and John Taylor, made the Niners' passing attack one of the best in the history of the game — Montana averaged nearly 10 yards for every pass attempt. But they could also run the ball — Roger Craig running for more than 1,000 yards. It surprised no one that they not only won the Super Bowl, but won handily, 55–10, over the Denver Broncos.

American Football League Champions
(before the Super Bowl era)

Year	Winner
1960	Houston Oilers
1961	Houston Oilers
1962	Dallas Texans
1963	San Diego Chargers
1964	Buffalo Bills
1965	Buffalo Bills

Great Teams:
The 1972 Miami Dolphins
Though some have felt their schedule was light, it's hard to improve on a perfect season — the only perfect season in NFL history. The Miami Dolphins featured such greats as Bob Griese, Mercury Morris, and Larry Czonka. Almost inexplicably, they were underdogs going into the Super Bowl, but silenced their critics with a 14–7 win over the Washington Redskins. Call them overrated if you will, but they beat all comers.

Great Teams:
The 1979 Pittsburgh Steelers
The names of the players on the 1979 Steelers speak volumes: Terry Bradshaw, Lynn Swann, John Stallworth, Franco Harris, "Mean" Joe Greene, Jack Lambert, and Jack Ham. The team had 10 Pro Bowlers, and after a 12–4 regular season breezed through the playoffs, ultimately winning the Super Bowl with a 31–19 win over the Los Angeles Rams. It was the second straight Super Bowl win for one of the most celebrated teams of their era.

NCAA National Champions

Prior to the Bowl Championship Series, National Champions were named by various polls. From 1936 to 1949, the Associated Press was the most widely recognized poll, and champions named by the AP for those years are listed in official NCAA records.

From 1950 to 1997, multiple polls existed: AP, UPI, FWAA,USA/CNN, and USA/ESPN. Champions selected by these polls are listed in NCAA records as "consensus" national champions. In several years polls disagreed, and for those years multiple champions are listed.

AP National Champions:

Year	Winner
1936	Minnesota
1937	Pittsburgh
1938	Texas Christian University
1939	Texas A&M
1940	Minnesota
1941	Minnesota
1942	Ohio State
1943	Notre Dame
1944	Army
1945	Army
1946	Notre Dame
1947	Notre Dame
1948	Michigan
1949	Notre Dame

Consensus National Champions:

Year	Winner
1950	Oklahoma
1951	Tennessee
1952	Michigan State
1953	Maryland
1954	University of California, Los Angeles
	Ohio State
1955	Oklahoma
1956	Oklahoma
1957	Ohio State
	Auburn
1958	Louisiana State University
	Iowa
1959	Syracuse
1960	Minnesota
	Mississippi
1961	Alabama
	Ohio State
1962	USC
1963	Texas
1964	Alabama
	Arkansas
	Notre Dame
1965	Michigan State
	Alabama
1966	Notre Dame
	Michigan State
1967	USC
1968	Ohio State
1969	Texas
1970	Nebraska
	Texas

	Ohio State
1971	Nebraska
1972	USC
1973	Notre Dame
	Alabama
1974	USC
	Oklahoma
1975	Oklahoma
1976	Pittsburgh
1977	Notre Dame
1978	Alabama
	USC
1979	Alabama
1980	Georgia
1981	Clemson
1982	Penn State
1983	Miami
1984	Brigham Young
1985	Oklahoma
1986	Penn State
1987	Miami
1988	Notre Dame
1989	Miami
1990	Colorado
	Georgia Tech
1991	Washington
	Miami
1992	Alabama
1993	Florida State
1994	Nebraska
1995	Nebraska
1996	Florida
1997	Michigan
	Nebraska
2003	USC

Bowl Championship Series Champions:

Year	Winner
1998	Tennessee
1999	Florida State
2000	Oklahoma
2001	Miami
2002	Ohio State
2003	Louisiana State
2004	USC
2005	Texas
2006	Florida
2007	Louisiana State
2008	Florida

Great Teams:
The 1971 Nebraska Cornhuskers
Wingback Johnny Rodgers thrilled fans with his kickoff and punt returns to help Nebraska to a 13–0 record and a National Championship in 1971. The team was phenomenal: they averaged 39 points a game on offence, and only eight points a game on defence. They were only seriously challenged once, when the number one ranked Huskers defeated the number two ranked Oklahoma Sooners 35–31 in what was dubbed the "Game of the Century."

Great Teams:
The 1972 USC Trojans
The 1972 edition of the Trojans may have been the greatest in the history of the school's storied football program. A perfect 12–0 season included a decisive win against Notre Dame, and a dismantling of Ohio State at the Rose Bowl. The strength of this team was a trio of running backs: Sam "Bam" Cunningham, Anthony Davis, and Rod McNeill.

Grey Cup Champions

Year	Winner
1909	University of Toronto Varsity Blues
1910	University of Toronto Varsity Blues
1911	University of Toronto Varsity Blues
1912	Hamilton Alerts
1913	Hamilton Tigers
1914	Toronto Argonauts
1915	Hamilton Tigers
1916	No game due to World War I
1917	No game due to World War I
1918	No game due to World War I
1919	No game due to influenza epidemic
1920	University of Toronto Varsity Blues
1921	Toronto Argonauts
1922	Queen's University
1923	Queen's University
1924	Queen's University
1925	Ottawa Senators
1926	Ottawa Senators
1927	Toronto Balmy Beach
1928	Hamilton Tigers
1929	Hamilton Tigers
1930	Toronto Balmy Beach
1931	Montreal AAA
1932	Hamilton Tigers
1933	Toronto Argonauts
1934	Sarnia Imperials
1935	Winnipeg 'Pegs
1936	Sarnia Imperials
1937	Toronto Argonauts

1938	Toronto Argonauts
1939	Winnipeg Blue Bombers
1940	Ottawa Rough Riders
1941	Winnipeg Blue Bombers
1942	Toronto RCAF Hurricanes
1943	Hamilton Flying Wildcats
1944	Montreal HMCS Donnacona
1945	Toronto Argonauts
1946	Toronto Argonauts
1947	Toronto Argonauts
1948	Calgary Stampeders
1949	Montreal Alouettes
1950	Toronto Argonauts
1951	Ottawa Rough Riders
1952	Toronto Argonauts
1953	Hamilton Tiger-Cats
1954	Edmonton Eskimos
1955	Edmonton Eskimos
1956	Edmonton Eskimos
1957	Hamilton Tiger-Cats
1958	Winnipeg Blue Bombers
1959	Winnipeg Blue Bombers
1960	Ottawa Rough Riders
1961	Winnipeg Blue Bombers
1962	Winnipeg Blue Bombers
1963	Hamilton Tiger-Cats
1964	B.C. Lions
1965	Hamilton Tiger-Cats
1966	Saskatchewan Roughriders
1967	Hamilton Tiger-Cats
1968	Ottawa Rough Riders
1969	Ottawa Rough Riders

1970	Montreal Alouettes
1971	Calgary Stampeders
1972	Hamilton Tiger-Cats
1973	Ottawa Rough Riders
1974	Montreal Alouettes
1975	Edmonton Eskimos
1976	Ottawa Rough Riders
1977	Montreal Alouettes
1978	Edmonton Eskimos
1979	Edmonton Eskimos
1980	Edmonton Eskimos
1981	Edmonton Eskimos
1982	Edmonton Eskimos
1983	Toronto Argonauts
1984	Winnipeg Blue Bombers
1985	B.C. Lions
1986	Hamilton Tiger-Cats
1987	Edmonton Eskimos
1988	Winnipeg Blue Bombers
1989	Saskatchewan Roughriders
1990	Winnipeg Blue Bombers
1991	Toronto Argonauts
1992	Calgary Stampeders
1993	Edmonton Eskimos
1994	B.C. Lions
1995	Baltimore Stallions
1996	Toronto Argonauts
1997	Toronto Argonauts
1998	Calgary Stampeders
1999	Hamilton Tiger-Cats
2000	B.C. Lions
2001	Calgary Stampeders

2002	Montreal Alouettes
2003	Edmonton Eskimos
2004	Toronto Argonauts
2005	Edmonton Eskimos
2006	B.C. Lions
2007	Saskatchewan Roughriders
2008	Calgary Stampeders

Great Teams:
The 1948 Calgary Stampeders

While the team is overshadowed in the history books by the wild celebration of Stamps fans at the Grey Cup, the team itself was phenomenal, featuring such legends as Normie Kwong, Paul Rowe, and Woody Strode. Their Grey Cup win capped off a perfect season.

Great Teams:
The 1981 Edmonton Eskimos

The Eskimos of the late 1970s and early 1980s were one of the great dynasties in football; winning five straight Grey Cups, thanks in large part to Warren Moon, one of the greatest quarterbacks ever to play the game. The 1981 Esks might have been the best team of that dynasty, finishing with a 14–1–1 record and winning one of the most memorable Grey Cup games ever played.

Great Teams:
The 1994 Toronto Argonauts

The line up was impressive: Paul Masotti, Pinball Clemons, Derrell Mitchell, Mike Vanderjagt, and a host of other tremendous players helped the team to a 15–3 record and a Grey Cup win. But the heart of the team may have been quarterback Doug Flutie, who dazzled fans with the brand of football that had come to be known as "Flutie Magic."

Vanier Cup Champions

Year	Winner
1965	University of Toronto Varsity Blues
1966	St. Francis Xavier University X-Men
1967	University of Alberta Golden Bears
1968	Queen's University Golden Gaels
1969	University of Manitoba Bisons
1970	University of Manitoba Bisons
1971	University of Western Ontario Mustangs
1972	University of Alberta Golden Bears
1973	St. Mary's University Huskies
1974	University of Western Ontario Mustangs
1975	University of Ottawa Gee-Gees
1976	University of Western Ontario Mustangs
1977	University of Western Ontario Mustangs
1978	Queen's University Golden Gaels
1979	Acadia University Axemen
1980	University of Alberta Golden Bears
1981	Acadia University Axemen
1982	University of British Columbia Thunderbirds
1983	University of Calgary Dinosaurs
1984	University of Guelph Gryphons
1985	University of Calgary Dinosaurs
1986	University of British Columbia Thunderbirds
1987	McGill University Redmen
1988	University of Calgary Dinosaurs
1989	University of Western Ontario Mustangs
1990	University of Saskatchewan Huskies
1991	Wilfrid Laurier University Golden Hawks
1992	Queen's University Golden Gaels

1993	University of Toronto Varsity Blues
1994	University of Western Ontario Mustangs
1995	University of Calgary Dinosaurs
1996	University of Saskatchewan Huskies
1997	University of British Columbia Thunderbirds
1998	University of Saskatchewan Huskies
1999	Université Laval Rouge et Or
2000	University of Ottawa Gee-Gees
2001	St. Mary's University Huskies
2002	St. Mary's University Huskies
2003	Université Laval Rouge et Or
2004	Université Laval Rouge et Or
2005	Wilfrid Laurier University Golden Hawks
2006	Université Laval Rouge et Or
2007	University of Manitoba Bisons
2008	Université Laval Rouge et Or

List of Arena Football League (ArenaBowl) Champions

Year	Winner
1987	Denver Dynamite
1988	Detroit Drive
1989	Detroit Drive
1990	Detroit Drive
1991	Tampa Bay Storm
1992	Detroit Drive
1993	Tampa Bay Storm
1994	Arizona Rattlers
1995	Tampa Bay Storm
1996	Tampa Bay Storm
1997	Arizona Rattlers

1998	Orlando Predators
1999	Albany Firebirds
2000	Orlando Predators
2001	Grand Rapids Portage
2002	San Jose SabreCats
2003	Tampa Bay Storm
2004	San Jose SabreCats
2005	Colorado Crush
2006	Chicago Rush
2007	San Jose SabreCats
2008	Philadelphia Soul

World Football League Champions

Year	Winner
1974	Birmingham Americans
1975*	Birmingham Vulcans

* The WFL folded before the 1975 season was completed, and the championship was awarded by virtue of win-loss records, without a playoff.

United States Football League Champions

Year	Winner
1983	Michigan Panthers
1984	Philadelphia Stars
1985	Baltimore Stars

World League of American Football / NFL Europe (World Bowl*) Champions

Year	Winner
1991	London Monarchs
1992	Sacramento Surge
1993	*No champion — league on hiatus*
1994	*No champion — league on hiatus*
1995	Frankfurt Galaxy
1996	Scottish Claymores
1997	Barcelona Dragons
1998	Rhein Fire
1999	Frankfurt Galaxy
2000	Rhein Fire
2001	Berlin Thunder
2002	Berlin Thunder
2003	Frankfurt Galaxy
2004	Berlin Thunder
2005	Amsterdam Admirals
2006	Frankfurt Galaxy
2007	Hamburg Sea Devils

* Though the championship trophy of the WLAF / NFL Europe was known as the "World Bowl," it should not be confused with the championship trophy of the World Football League, which was also known as the "World Bowl."

question
and feature list

Gridiron History

Football in Media and Popular Culture

Rules and Lingo

Strategy and Plays

Legends, Characters, and Heroes

Great and Not-So-Great Moments

Firsts and Record-Breakers

Leagues of the Past

The Fab Forty: The Greatest Plays in Football

Champions

Other Books in the Now You Know Series

**Now You Know
Soccer**
978-1-55488-416-2
$19.99

**Now You Know
Golf**
978-1-55002-870-6
$19.99

**Now You Know
Hockey**
978-1-55002-869-0
$19.99

**Now You Know
Big Book of Sports**
978-1-55488-454-4
$29.99

**Now You Know
Big Book of Answers**
978-1-55002-741-9
$29.99

**Now You Know
Big Book of Answers 2**
978-1-55002-871-3
$29.99

More Books in the Now You Know Series

Now You Know Canada's Heroes 978-1-55488-444-5 $19.99
Now You Know Royalty 978-1-55488-415-5 $19.99
Now You Know Disasters 978-1-55002-807-2 $9.99
Now You Know Pirates 978-1-55002-806-5 $9.99
Now You Know Extreme Weather 978-1-55002-743-3 $9.99
Now You Know Christmas 978-1-55002-745-7 $9.99
Now You Know Crime Scenes 978-1-55002-774-7 $9.99
Now You Know 978-1-55002-461-6 $19.99
Now You Know More 978-1-55002-530-9 $19.99
Now You Know Almost Everything 978-1-55002-575-0 $19.99
Now You Know Volume 4 978-1-55002-648-1 $19.99

Available at your favourite bookseller.

DUNDURN PRESS
www.dundurn.com

Did Now You Know satiate your desire for little-known facts, or do you want more? Visit *www.nowyouknow.com*, sign up for the Answer of the Week, and have a little-known fact delivered straight into your inbox!